I U.S. Military Deployment

Other Books in the At Issue Series:

U.S. Military Deployment

Noël Merino, Book Editor

GREENHAVEN PRESS
A part of Gale, Cengage Learning

Detroit • New York • San Francisco • New Haven, Conn • Waterville, Maine • London

Christine Nasso, *Publisher*
Elizabeth Des Chenes, *Managing Editor*

© 2010 Greenhaven Press, a part of Gale, Cengage Learning.

Gale and Greenhaven Press are registered trademarks used herein under license.

For more information, contact:
Greenhaven Press
27500 Drake Rd.
Farmington Hills, MI 48331-3535
Or you can visit our Internet site at gale.cengage.com

For product information and technology assistance, contact us at

Gale Customer Support, 1-800-877-4253
For permission to use material from this text or product, submit all requests online at www.cengage.com/permissions.

Further permissions questions can be e-mailed to permissionrequest@cengage.com.

Articles in Greenhaven Press anthologies are often edited for length to meet page requirements. In addition, original titles of these works are changed to clearly present the main thesis and to explicitly indicate the author's opinion. Every effort is made to ensure that Greenhaven Press accurately reflects the original intent of the authors. Every effort has been made to trace the owners of copyrighted material.

Cover Image copyright Stocktrek/Brand X Pictures/Getty Images.

LIBRARY OF CONGRESS CATALOGING-IN-PUBLICATION DATA

U.S. military deployment / Noël Merino, book editor.
    p. cm. -- (At issue)
    Includes bibliographical references and index.
    ISBN 978-0-7377-5373-8 (hardcover) -- ISBN 978-0-7377-5411-7 (pbk.)
    1. United States--Military policy--21st century--Public opinion. 2. United States--Foreign relations--1989---Public opinion. 3. Intervention (International law)--Public opinion. 4. War--Public opinion. 5. Public opinion--United States. I. Merino, Noël.
        UA23.U224 2010
        355.4'73--dc22
                                                                    2010029232

Printed in the United States of America
1 2 3 4 5 6 7 14 13 12 11 10

Contents

Introduction

The president of the United States heads the U.S. military, with military policy carried out by the U.S. Department of Defense (DoD). The U.S. Armed Forces branches—the Army, Air Force, Navy, and Marine Corps—are under the direction of the DoD. As of 2010 the United States spends approximately $700 billion annually for its national defense. The U.S. military is the second largest in the world (after China), with 1.4 million people on active duty and 800,000 in the reserves, as of the end of 2009. At the same time there were 151,000 troops deployed in and around Iraq, including Kuwait, and 71,000 troops in and around Afghanistan. Outside of these two countries there were a total of 284,100 troops dispersed around the world.[1]

A large number of the troops deployed around the world outside of the active wars in Iraq and Afghanistan are located at the U.S. military bases created after the Allies defeated the Axis powers in World War II. To this day, the United States has a strong military presence in the former Axis countries of Germany, Japan, and Italy: At the end of 2009, there were 52,440 troops and 235 U.S. military sites in Germany; 35,688 troops and 123 U.S. military sites in Japan; and 9,660 troops and 83 sites in Italy.[2] The U.S. military presence in Japan is the result of the U.S.–Japan Treaty of Mutual Cooperation and Security. A similar situation occurred following U.S. involvement in the Korean War. Under the 1953 U.S.–R.O.K.

1. Department of Defense, "Active Duty Military Personnel Strengths by Regional Area and by Country," December 31, 2009. http://siadapp.dmdc.osd.mil/personnel/MILITARY/history/hst0912.pdf.
2. Department of Defense, "Active Duty Military Personnel Strengths by Regional Area and by Country," December 31, 2009. http://siadapp.dmdc.osd.mil/personnel/MILITARY/history/hst0912.pdf AND Department of Defense, Base Structure Report, Fiscal Year 2009 Baseline, September 2009. http://www.acq.osd.mil/ie/download/bsr/BSR2009Baseline.pdf.

Mutual Defense Treaty, the United States agreed to help the Republic of Korea (R.O.K.)—or South Korea—defend itself. Since then, the United States has maintained military personnel in South Korea. At the end of 2009, there were approximately 28,500 troops and 87 sites in South Korea.

The U.S. policy regarding military deployment at foreign bases has been shifting in recent years. The Global Posture Review, a base realignment process started in the George W. Bush Administration, made plans to reshape America's global military base network. According to the plan, approximately 70,000 U.S. military personnel would return to the United States over a ten-year implementation period—about a quarter of those currently deployed outside of the wars in Iraq and Afghanistan. The total number of American military sites abroad would decline by about 35 percent over that same ten-year period.[3]

Some of the base realignments have begun, with U.S. military forces leaving Western Europe in recent years. Other changes have occurred in Asia: In February 2009 Secretary of State Hillary Clinton and then-Foreign Minister Hirofumi Nakasone signed the Guam International Agreement (GIA), committing both nations to complete the transfer of approximately 8,000 U.S. Marines from bases in Okinawa to new facilities in Guam built with the assistance of Japan. Following the 2009 election in Japan, the new government pledged to review the existing agreement and negotiations are still underway. Additionally, in 2004, the United States and South Korea agreed to reduce the number of U.S. troops to 25,000 by 2008, but a subsequent agreement in 2008 capped that number at 28,500, with no further troop reductions planned. The United States and South Korea have also agreed to transfer wartime operational control to the R.O.K. military on April 17, 2012.

3. Department of Defense, "Strengthening U.S. Global Defense Posture," September 2004. www.dmzhawaii.org/wp-content/uploads/2008/12/global_posture.pdf.

The future presence of the U.S. military at foreign military bases and in wartime deployment depends on the military strategy of the Obama Administration. In May 2010 the White House laid out the national security strategy for the coming years. In the introduction, President Barack Obama emphasized that the United States "will maintain the military superiority that has secured our country, and underpinned global security, for decades." But, the White House cautions, "when we overuse our military might, or fail to invest in or deploy complementary tools, or act without partners, then our military is overstretched, Americans bear a greater burden, and our leadership around the world is too narrowly identified with military force."[4] The debate will surely continue about the proper role for the United States in global security issues. Should the United States continue its military presence in Afghanistan and Iraq? Should the United States continue to have a widespread presence throughout the world through deployment at foreign military bases? Varied answers to these and other questions are covered within the viewpoints included in *At Issue: U.S. Military Deployment.*

4. White House, National Security Strategy, 2010. http://www.whitehouse.gov/sites/default/files/rss_viewer/national_security_strategy.pdf.

1

U.S. Military Presence Around the World Is Expanding Despite Protests

Catherine Lutz

In the following viewpoint Catherine Lutz contends that the U.S. military has a vast worldwide presence that continues to expand. She argues that World War II laid the groundwork for the development of thousands of U.S. military bases around the globe, an expansion of military power that has continued for several decades. Lutz claims that the aggressiveness with which the United States has pursued global military expansion has increased in recent years, shifting from a solely defensive strategy to one that is now also offensive. Many of the arguments in favor of U.S. military bases abroad are problematic, Lutz asserts. There are numerous protests overseas regarding the existence of U.S. bases, but the expansion continues unabated. Lutz is a professor at the Watson Institute of International Studies at Brown University and editor of The Bases of Empire: The Global Struggle Against U.S. Military Posts.

In December 2008, shortly before being sworn in as the forty-fourth president of the United States, Barack Obama pledged his belief that, "to ensure prosperity here at home and peace abroad", it was vital to maintain "the strongest military on the planet". Unveiling his national security team, including George Bush's defence secretary, Robert Gates, he said: "We also agree the strength of our military has to be combined

Catherine Lutz, "Obama's Empire," *New Statesman (1996)*, vol. 138, August 3, 2009, pp. 22–27. Copyright © 2009 New Statesman, Ltd. Reproduced by permission.

with the wisdom and force of diplomacy, and that we are going to be committed to rebuilding and restrengthening alliances around the world to advance American interests and American security."

The Global Reach of the U.S. Military

Unfortunately, many of the Obama administration's diplomatic efforts are being directed towards maintaining and garnering new access for the US military across the globe. US military officials, through their Korean proxies, have completed the eviction of resistant rice farmers from their land around Camp Humphreys, South Korea, for its expansion (including a new 18-hole golf course); they are busily making back-room deals with officials in the Northern Mariana Islands to gain the use of the Pacific islands there for bombing and training purposes; and they are scrambling to express support for a regime in Kyrgyzstan that has been implicated in the murder of its political opponents but whose Manas Airbase, used to stage US military actions in Afghanistan since 2001, Obama and the Pentagon consider crucial for the expanded war there.

The global reach of the US military today is unprecedented and unparalleled. Officially, more than 190,000 troops and 115,000 civilian employees are massed in approximately 900 military facilities in 46 countries and territories (the unofficial figure is far greater). The US military owns or rents 795,000 acres of land, with 26,000 buildings and structures, valued at $146bn (£89bn). The bases bristle with an inventory of weapons whose worth is measured in the trillions and whose killing power could wipe out all life on earth several times over.

The official figures exclude the huge build-up of troops and structures in Iraq and Afghanistan over the past decade, as well as secret or unacknowledged facilities in Israel, Kuwait, the Philippines and many other places. In just three years of the Iraq and Afghanistan wars, £2bn was spent on military construction. A single facility in Iraq, Balad Airbase, houses 30,000 troops and 10,000 contractors, and extends across 16 square miles, with an additional 12 square mile "security perimeter".

From the battle zones of Afghanistan and Iraq to quiet corners of Curaçao, Korea and Britain, the US military domain consists of sprawling army bases, small listening posts, missile and artillery testing ranges and berthed aircraft carriers (moved to "trouble spots" around the world, each carrier is considered by the US navy as "four and a half acres of sovereign US territory"). While the bases are, literally speaking, barracks and weapons depots, staging areas for war-making and ship repairs, complete with golf courses and basketball courts, they are also political claims, spoils of war, arms sale showrooms and toxic industrial sites. In addition to the cultural imperialism and episodes of rape, murder, looting and land seizure that have always accompanied foreign armies, local communities are now subjected to the ear-splitting noise of jets on exercise, to the risk of helicopters and warplanes crashing into residential areas, and to exposure to the toxic materials that the military uses in its daily operations.

The Rapid Worldwide Expansion of U.S. Bases

The global expansion of US bases—and with it the rise of the US as a world superpower—is a legacy of the Second World War. In 1938, the US had 14 military bases outside its continental borders. Seven years later, it had 30,000 installations in roughly 100 countries. While this number was projected to shrink to 2,000 by 1948 (following pressure from other nations to return bases in their own territory or colonies, and pressure at home to demobilise the 12-million-man military), the US continued to pursue access rights to land and air space around the world. It established security alliances with multiple states within Europe (NATO) [North Atlantic Treaty Organization], the Middle East and south Asia (CENTO) [Central Treaty Organization] and south-east Asia (SEATO) [Southeast Asia Treaty Organization], as well as bilateral agreements with Japan, Taiwan, South Korea, Australia and New Zealand. Status of Forces Agreements (SOFAs) were crafted in each country to specify what the military could do, and usually gave US soldiers broad immunity from prosecution for crimes committed and environmental damage caused. These agreements and subsequent base operations have mostly been shrouded in secrecy, helped by the National Security Act of 1947. New US bases were built in remarkable numbers in West Germany, Italy, Britain and Japan, with the defeated Axis powers hosting the most significant numbers (at one point, Japan was peppered with 3,800 US installations).

As battles become bases, so bases become battles; the sites in east Asia acquired during the Spanish-American War in 1898 and during the Second World War—such as Guam, Thailand and the Philippines—became the primary bases from which the US waged war on Vietnam. The number of raids over north and south Vietnam required tons of bombs unloaded at the naval station in Guam. The morale of ground troops based in Vietnam, as fragile as it was to become through the latter part of the 1960s, depended on R&R (rest and recreation) at bases outside the country, which allowed them to leave the war zone and yet be shipped back quickly and inexpensively for further fighting. The war also depended on the heroin the CIA [Central Intelligence Agency] was able to ship in to the troops on the battlefield in Vietnam from its secret bases in Laos. By 1967, the number of US bases had returned to 1947 levels.

The Impact of Technology

Technological changes in warfare have had important effects on the configuration of US bases. Long-range missiles and the development of ships that can make much longer runs with-

The worldwide presence of the U.S. military continues to expand. These servicemen are stationed at an airbase in Kyrgystan. AP Images.

out resupply have altered the need for a line of bases to move forces forward into combat zones, as has the aerial refuelling of military jets. An arms airlift from the US to the British in the Middle East in 1941–42, for example, required a long hopscotch of bases, from Florida to Cuba, Puerto Rico, Barbados, Trinidad, British Guiana, northeast Brazil, Fernando de Noronha, Takoradi (now in Ghana), Lagos, Kano (now in Nigeria) and Khartoum, before finally making delivery in Egypt. In the early 1970s, US aircraft could make the same delivery with one stop in the Azores, and today can do so nonstop.

On the other hand, the pouring of money into military R&D [research and development] (the Pentagon has spent more than $85bn in 2009), and the corporate profits to be made in the development and deployment of the resulting technologies, have been significant factors in the ever larger numbers of technical facilities on foreign soil. These include such things as missile early-warning radar, signals intelligence, satellite control and space-tracking telescopes. The will to gain military control of space, as well as gather intelligence, has led to the establishment of numerous new military bases in violation of arms-control agreements such as the 1967 Outer Space Treaty. In Colombia and Peru, and in secret and mobile locations elsewhere in Latin America, radar stations are primarily used for anti-trafficking operations.

A Change in U.S. Military Strategy

Since 2000, with the election of George W. Bush and the ascendancy to power of a group of men who believed in a more aggressive and unilateral use of military power (some of whom stood to profit handsomely from the increased military budget that would require), US imperial ambition has grown. Following the declaration of a war on terror and of the right to preemptive war, the number of countries into which the US inserted and based troops radically expanded. The Pentagon put into action a plan for a network of "deployment" or "forward operating" bases to increase the reach of current and future forces. The Pentagon-aligned, neoconservative think tank the Project for the New American Century stressed that "while the unresolved conflict with Iraq provides the immediate justification, the need for a substantial American force presence in the Gulf transcends the issue of the regime of Saddam Hussein".

The new bases are designed to operate not defensively against particular threats but as offensive, expeditionary platforms from which military capabilities can be projected quickly, anywhere. The Global Defence Posture Review of 2004 announced these changes, focusing not just on reorienting the footprint of US bases away from cold war locations, but on remaking legal arrangements that support expanded military activities with other allied countries and prepositioning equipment in those countries. As a recent army strategic document notes, "Military personnel can be transported to, and fall in on, prepositioned equipment significantly more quickly than the equivalent unit could be transported to the theatre, and prepositioning equipment overseas is generally less politically difficult than stationing US military personnel."

Types of U.S. Military Bases

Terms such as facility, outpost or station are used for smaller bases to suggest a less permanent presence. The US department of defence currently distinguishes between three types of military facility. "Main operating bases" are those with permanent personnel, strong infrastructure, and often family housing, such as Kadena Airbase in Japan and Ramstein Airbase in Germany. "Forward operating sites" are "expandable warm facilit[ies] maintained with a limited US military support presence and possibly prepositioned equipment", such as Incirlik Airbase in Turkey and Soto Cano Airbase in Honduras. Finally, "co-operative security locations" are sites with few or no permanent US personnel, maintained by contractors or the host nation for occasional use by the US military, and often referred to as "lily pads". These are cropping up around the world, especially throughout Africa, a recent example being in Dakar, Senegal.

Moreover, these bases are the anchor—and merely the most visible aspect—of the US military's presence overseas. Every year, US forces train 100,000 soldiers in 180 countries, the presumption being that beefed-up local militaries will help to pursue US interests in local conflicts and save the US money, casualties and bad publicity when human rights abuses occur (the blowback effect of such activities has been made clear by the strength of the Taliban since 9/11). The US military presence also involves jungle, urban, desert, maritime and polar training exercises across wide swathes of landscape, which have become the pretext for substantial and permanent positioning of troops. In recent years, the US has run around 20 exercises annually on Philippine soil, which have resulted in a near-continuous presence of US soldiers in a country whose people ejected US bases in 1992 and whose constitution forbids foreign troops to be based on its territory. Finally, US personnel work every day to shape local legal codes to facilitate US access: they have lobbied, for example, to change the Philippine and Japanese constitutions to allow, respectively, foreign troop basing and a more-than-defensive military.

The Arguments for U.S. Military Bases

Asked why the US has a vast network of military bases around the world, Pentagon officials give both utilitarian and humanitarian arguments. Utilitarian arguments include the claim that bases provide security for the US by deterring attack from hostile countries and preventing or remedying unrest or military challenges; that bases serve the national economic interests of the US, ensuring access to markets and commodities needed to maintain US standards of living; and that bases are symbolic markers of US power and credibility—and so the more the better. Humanitarian arguments present bases as altruistic gifts to other nations, helping to liberate or democratise them, or offering aid relief. None of these humanitarian arguments deals with the problem that many of the bases were taken during wartime and "given" to the US by another of the war's victors.

Critics of US foreign policy have dissected and dismantled the arguments made for maintaining a global system of military basing. They have shown that the bases have often failed in their own terms: despite the Pentagon's claims that they provide security to the regions they occupy, most of the world's people feel anything but reassured by their presence. Instead of providing more safety for the US or its allies, they have often provoked attacks, and have made the communities around bases key targets of other nation's missiles. On the island of Belau in the Pacific, the site of sharp resistance to US attempts to instal a submarine base and jungle training centre, people describe their experience of military basing in the Second World War: "When soldiers come, war comes." On Guam, a joke among locals is that few people except for nuclear strategists in the Kremlin know where their island is.

As for the argument that bases serve the national economic interest of the US, the weapons, personnel and fossil fuels involved cost billions of dollars, most coming from US taxpayers. While bases have clearly been concentrated in countries with key strategic resources, particularly along the routes of oil and gas pipelines in central Asia, the Middle East and, increasingly, Africa, from which one-quarter of US oil imports are expected by 2015, the profits have gone first of all to the corporations that build and service them, such as Halliburton. The myth that bases are an altruistic form of "foreign aid" for locals is exploded by the substantial costs involved for host economies and polities. The immediate negative effects include levels of pollution, noise, crime and lost productive land that cannot be offset by soldiers' local spending or employment of local people. Other putative gains tend to benefit only local elites and further militarise the host nations: elaborate bilateral negotiations swap weapons, cash and trade privileges for overflight and land-use rights. Less explicitly, rice imports, immigration rights to the US or overlooking human rights abuses have been the currency of exchange.

The environmental, political, and economic impact of these bases is enormous. The social problems that accompany bases, including soldiers' violence against women and car crashes, have to be handled by local communities without compensation from the US. Some communities pay the highest price: their farmland taken for bases, their children neurologically damaged by military jet fuel in their water supplies, their neighbours imprisoned, tortured and disappeared by the autocratic regimes that survive on US military and political support given as a form of tacit rent for the bases. The US military has repeatedly interfered in the domestic affairs of nations in which it has or desires military access, operating to influence votes and undermine or change local laws that stand in the way.

Protests of U.S. Bases

Social movements have proliferated around the world in response to the empire of US bases, ever since its inception. The attempt to take the Philippines from Spain in 1898 led to a drawn-out guerrilla war for independence that required 126,000 US occupation troops to stifle. Between 1947 and 1990, the US military was asked to leave France, Yugoslavia, Iran, Ethiopia, Libya, Sudan, Saudi Arabia, Tunisia, Algeria, Vietnam, Indonesia, Peru, Mexico and Venezuela. Popular and political objection to the bases in Spain, the Philippines, Greece and Turkey in the 1980s gave those governments the grounds to negotiate significantly more compensation from the US. Portugal threatened to evict the US from important bases in the Azores unless it ceased its support for independence for its African colonies.

Since 1990, the US has been sent packing, most significantly, from the Philippines, Panama, Saudi Arabia, Vieques and Uzbekistan. Of its own accord, for varying reasons, it decided to leave countries from Ghana to Fiji. Persuading the US to clean up after itself—including, in Panama, more than 100,000 rounds of unexploded ordnance—is a further struggle. As in the case of the US navy's removal from Vieques in 2003, arguments about the environmental and health damage of the military's activities remain the centrepiece of resistance to bases.

Many are also concerned by other countries' overseas bases—primarily European, Russian and Chinese—and by the activities of their own militaries, but the far greater number of US bases and their weaponry has understandably been the focus. The sense that US bases represent a major injustice to the host community and nation is very strong in countries where

US bases have the longest standing and are most ubiquitous. In Okinawa, polls show that 70 to 80 per cent of the island's people want the bases, or at least the marines, to leave. In 1995, the abduction and rape of a 12-year-old Okinawan girl by two US marines and one US sailor led to demands for the removal of all US bases in Japan. One family in Okinawa has built a large peace museum right up against the edge of the Futenma Airbase, with a stairway to the roof that allows busloads of schoolchildren and other visitors to view the sprawling base after looking at art depicting the horrors of war.

In Korea, the great majority of the population feels that a reduction in US presence would increase national security; in recent years, several violent deaths at the hands of US soldiers triggered vast candlelight vigils and protests across the country. And the original inhabitants of Diego Garcia, evicted from their homes between 1967 and 1973 by the British on behalf of the US for a naval base, have organised a concerted campaign for the right to return, bringing legal suit against the British government, a story told in David Vine's recent book *Island of Shame*. There is also resistance to the US expansion plans into new areas. In 2007, a number of African nations baulked at US attempts to secure access to sites for military bases. In eastern Europe, despite well-funded campaigns to convince Poles and Czechs of the value of US bases and much sentiment in favour of accepting them in pursuit of closer ties with NATO and the EU [European Union], and promised economic benefits, vigorous protests have included hunger strikes and led the Czech government, in March [2009], to reverse its plan to allow a US military radar base to be built in the country.

The U.S. Response to Protests

The US has responded to action against bases with a renewed emphasis on "force protection", in some cases enforcing curfews on soldiers, and cutting back on events that bring local people on to base property. The department of defence has also engaged in the time-honoured practice of renaming: clusters of soldiers, buildings and equipment have become "defence staging posts" or "forward operating locations" rather than military bases. Regulating documents become "visiting forces agreements", not "status of forces agreements", or remain entirely secret. While major reorganisation of bases is under way for a host of reasons, including a desire to create a more mobile force with greater access to the Middle East, eastern Europe and central Asia, the motives also include an attempt to prevent political momentum of the sort that ended US use of the Vieques and Philippine bases.

The attempt to gain permanent basing in Iraq foundered in 2008 on the objections of forces in both Iraq and the US. Obama, in his Cairo speech in June [2009], may have insisted that "we pursue no bases" in either Iraq or Afghanistan, but there has been no sign of any significant dismantling of bases there, or of scaling back the US military presence in the rest of the world. The US secretary of state, Hillary Clinton, recently visited Japan to ensure that it follows through on promises to provide the US with a new airfield on Okinawa and billions of dollars to build new housing and other facilities for 8,000 marines relocating to Guam. She ignored the invitation of island activists to come and see the damage left by previous decades of US base activities. The myriad land-grabs and hundreds of billions of dollars spent to quarter troops around the world persist far beyond Iraq and Afghanistan, and too far from the headlines.

2

The U.S. Military Presence Around the World Is Essential for Security

Bradley A. Thayer

In the following viewpoint Bradley Thayer argues that the United States must continue its foreign policy based on American primacy. He contends that maintaining U.S. power works to protect American interests around the globe, requiring a worldwide military presence. This power ensures that most nations will want to be aligned with the United States, a circumstance that promotes world peace. Thayer claims that there are numerous other benefits of primacy besides international peace, including the promotion of democracy, global economic growth, and improved welfare of people worldwide. As such, he concludes that American primacy must continue. Thayer is professor of political science at Baylor University, editor of Debates in International Relations, *and co-author—with Christopher Layne—of* American Empire: A Debate.

A grand strategy based on American primacy means ensuring the United States stays the world's number one power—the diplomatic, economic and military leader. Those arguing against primacy claim that the United States should retrench, either because the United States lacks the power to maintain its primacy and should withdraw from its global commitments, or because the maintenance of primacy will lead the United States into the trap of "imperial overstretch."

Bradley A. Thayer, "In Defense of Primacy," *National Interest*, November–December 2006, pp. 32–37. Copyright © The National Interest 2006, Washington, D.C. Reproduced by permission.

In the previous issue [Sept./Oct. 2006] of *The National Interest*, Christopher Layne warned of these dangers of primacy and called for retrenchment.

The Debate About Primacy and Retrenchment

Those arguing for a grand strategy of retrenchment are a diverse lot. They include isolationists, who want no foreign military commitments; selective engagers, who want U.S. military commitments to centers of economic might; and offshore balancers, who want a modified form of selective engagement that would have the United States abandon its landpower presence abroad in favor of relying on airpower and seapower to defend its interests.

But retrenchment, in any of its guises, must be avoided. If the United States adopted such a strategy, it would be a profound strategic mistake that would lead to far greater instability and war in the world, imperil American security and deny the United States and its allies the benefits of primacy.

There are two critical issues in any discussion of America's grand strategy: *Can* America remain the dominant state? *Should* it strive to do this? America can remain dominant due to its prodigious military, economic and soft power capabilities. The totality of that equation of power answers the first issue. The United States has overwhelming military capabilities and wealth in comparison to other states or likely potential alliances. Barring some disaster or tremendous folly, that will remain the case for the foreseeable future. With few exceptions, even those who advocate retrenchment acknowledge this.

So the debate revolves around the desirability of maintaining American primacy. Proponents of retrenchment focus a great deal on the costs of U.S. action—but they fail to realize what is good about American primacy. The price and risks of primacy are reported in newspapers every day; the benefits that stem from it are not.

The Protection of American Interests

A grand strategy of ensuring American primacy takes as its starting point the protection of the U.S. homeland and American global interests. These interests include ensuring that critical resources like oil flow around the world, that the global trade and monetary regimes flourish and that Washington's worldwide network of allies is reassured and protected. Allies are a great asset to the United States, in part because they shoulder some of its burdens. Thus, it is no surprise to see NATO [North Atlantic Treaty Organization] in Afghanistan or the Australians in East Timor.

In contrast, a strategy based on retrenchment will not be able to achieve these fundamental objectives of the United States. Indeed, retrenchment will make the United States less secure than the present grand strategy of primacy. This is because threats will exist no matter what role America chooses to play in international politics. Washington cannot call a "time out", and it cannot hide from threats. Whether they are terrorists, rogue states or rising powers, history shows that threats must be confronted. Simply by declaring that the United States is "going home", thus abandoning its commitments or making unconvincing half-pledges to defend its interests and allies, does not mean that others will respect American wishes to retreat. To make such a declaration implies weakness and emboldens aggression. In the anarchic world of the animal kingdom, predators prefer to eat the weak rather than confront the strong. The same is true of the anarchic world of international politics. If there is no diplomatic solution to the threats that confront the United States, then the conventional and strategic military power of the United States is what protects the country from such threats.

The Importance of Foreign Allies

And when enemies must be confronted, a strategy based on primacy focuses on engaging enemies overseas, away from

American soil. Indeed, a key tenet of the Bush Doctrine [named for President George W. Bush], is to attack terrorists far from America's shores and not to wait while they use bases in other countries to plan and train for attacks against the United States itself. This requires a physical, on-the-ground presence that cannot be achieved by offshore balancing.

Indeed, as Barry Posen [professor of political science] has noted, U.S. primacy is secured because America, at present, commands the "global commons"—the oceans, the world's airspace and outer space—allowing the United States to project its power far from its borders, while denying those common avenues to its enemies. As a consequence, the costs of power projection for the United States and its allies are reduced, and the robustness of the United States' conventional and strategic deterrent capabilities is increased. This is not an advantage that should be relinquished lightly.

A remarkable fact about international politics today—in a world where American primacy is clearly and unambiguously on display—is that countries want to align themselves with the United States. Of course, this is not out of any sense of altruism, in most cases, but because doing so allows them to use the power of the United States for their own purposes—their own protection, or to gain greater influence.

Of 192 countries, 84 are allied with America—their security is tied to the United States through treaties and other informal arrangements—and they include almost all of the major economic and military powers. That is a ratio of almost 17 to one (85 to five), and a big change from the Cold War when the ratio was about 1.8 to one of states aligned with the United States versus the Soviet Union. Never before in its history has this country, or any country, had so many allies.

U.S. Influence in International Politics

U.S. primacy—and the bandwagoning effect—has also given us extensive influence in international politics, allowing the

Thayer argues that the United States' military power is what put Iraq on the path to democracy. The first free elections in Iraq were held in 2005. AP Images.

United States to shape the behavior of states and international institutions. Such influence comes in many forms, one of which is America's ability to create coalitions of like-minded states to free Kosovo, stabilize Afghanistan, invade Iraq or to stop proliferation through the Proliferation Security Initiative (PSI). Doing so allows the United States to operate with allies outside of the UN [United Nations] where it can be stymied by opponents. American-led wars in Kosovo, Afghanistan and Iraq stand in contrast to the UN's inability to save the people of Darfur or even to conduct any military campaign to realize the goals of its charter. The quiet effectiveness of the PSI in dismantling Libya's WMD [weapons of mass destruction] programs and unraveling the A.Q. Khan [Pakistani scientist regarded as leader of Pakistan's nuclear program] proliferation network are in sharp relief to the typically toothless attempts by the UN to halt proliferation.

You can count with one hand countries opposed to the United States. They are the "Gang of Five": China, Cuba, Iran,

North Korea and Venezuela. Of course, countries like India, for example, do not agree with all policy choices made by the United States, such as toward Iran, but New Delhi is friendly to Washington. Only the "Gang of Five" may be expected to consistently resist the agenda and actions of the United States.

China is clearly the most important of these states because it is a rising great power. But even Beijing is intimidated by the United States and refrains from openly challenging U.S. power. China proclaims that it will, if necessary, resort to other mechanisms of challenging the United States, including asymmetric strategies such as targeting communication and intelligence satellites upon which the United States depends. But China may not be confident those strategies would work, and so it is likely to refrain from testing the United States directly for the foreseeable future because China's power benefits, as we shall see, from the international order U.S. primacy creates.

The other states are far weaker than China. For three of the "Gang of Five" cases—Venezuela, Iran, Cuba—it is an anti-U.S. regime that is the source of the problem; the country itself is not intrinsically anti-American. Indeed, a change of regime in Caracas, Tehran or Havana could very well reorient relations.

The Benefits of U.S. Power

Throughout history, peace and stability have been great benefits of an era where there was a dominant power—Rome, Britain or the United States today. Scholars and statesmen have long recognized the irenic [peace-promoting] effect of power on the anarchic world of international politics.

Everything we think of when we consider the current international order—free trade, a robust monetary regime, increasing respect for human rights, growing democratization—is directly linked to U.S. power. Retrenchment proponents seem to think that the current system can be maintained without the current amount of U.S. power behind it. In that they are dead wrong and need to be reminded of one of history's most significant lessons: Appalling things happen when international orders collapse. The Dark Ages followed Rome's collapse. Hitler succeeded the order established at Versailles. Without U.S. power, the liberal order created by the United States will end just as assuredly. As country and western great Ral Donner sang: "You don't know what you've got (until you lose it)."

Consequently, it is important to note what those good things are. In addition to ensuring the security of the United States and its allies, American primacy within the international system causes many positive outcomes for Washington and the world. The first has been a more peaceful world. During the Cold War, U.S. leadership reduced friction among many states that were historical antagonists, most notably France and West Germany. Today, American primacy helps keep a number of complicated relationships aligned—between Greece and Turkey, Israel and Egypt, South Korea and Japan, India and Pakistan, Indonesia and Australia. This is not to say it fulfills Woodrow Wilson's vision of ending all war. Wars still occur where Washington's interests are not seriously threatened, such as in Darfur, but a Pax Americana [American Peace] does reduce war's likelihood, particularly war's worst form: great power wars.

The Spread of Democracy

Second, American power gives the United States the ability to spread democracy and other elements of its ideology of liberalism. Doing so is a source of much good for the countries concerned as well as the United States because, as John Owen noted on these pages in the Spring 2006 issue, liberal democracies are more likely to align with the United States and be sympathetic to the American worldview. So, spreading democracy helps maintain U.S. primacy. In addition, once states are governed democratically, the likelihood of any type of conflict is significantly reduced. This is not because democracies do not have clashing interests. Indeed they do. Rather, it is because they are more open, more transparent and more likely to want to resolve things amicably in concurrence with U.S. leadership. And so, in general, democratic states are good for their citizens as well as for advancing the interests of the United States.

Critics have faulted the [George W.] Bush Administration for attempting to spread democracy in the Middle East, labeling such an effort a modern form of tilting at windmills. It is the obligation of Bush's critics to explain why democracy is good enough for Western states but not for the rest, and, one gathers from the argument, should not even be attempted.

Of course, whether democracy in the Middle East will have a peaceful or stabilizing influence on America's interests in the short run is open to question. Perhaps democratic Arab states would be more opposed to Israel, but nonetheless, their people would be better off. The United States has brought democracy to Afghanistan, where 8.5 million Afghans, 40 percent of them women, voted in a critical October 2004 election, even though remnant Taliban forces threatened them. The first free elections were held in Iraq in January 2005. It was the military power of the United States that put Iraq on the path to democracy. Washington fostered democratic governments in Europe, Latin America, Asia and the Caucasus. Now even the Middle East is increasingly democratic. They may not yet look like Western-style democracies, but democratic progress has been made in Algeria, Morocco, Lebanon, Iraq, Kuwait, the Palestinian Authority and Egypt. By all accounts, the march of democracy has been impressive.

The Growth of the Global Economy

Third, along with the growth in the number of democratic states around the world has been the growth of the global

economy. With its allies, the United States has labored to create an economically liberal worldwide network characterized
by free trade and commerce, respect for international property
rights, and mobility of capital and labor markets. The economic stability and prosperity that stems from this economic
order is a global public good from which all states benefit,
particularly the poorest states in the Third World. The United
States created this network not out of altruism but for the
benefit and the economic well-being of America. This economic order forces American industries to be competitive,
maximizes efficiencies and growth, and benefits defense as
well because the size of the economy makes the defense burden manageable. Economic spin-offs foster the development
of military technology, helping to ensure military prowess.

Perhaps the greatest testament to the benefits of the economic network comes from Deepak Lal, a former Indian foreign service diplomat and researcher at the World Bank, who
started his career confident in the socialist ideology of post-
independence India. Abandoning the positions of his youth,
Lal now recognizes that the only way to bring relief to desperately poor countries of the Third World is through the adop-
tion of free market economic policies and globalization, which
are facilitated through American primacy. As a witness to the
failed alternative economic systems, Lal is one of the strongest
academic proponents of American primacy due to the economic prosperity it provides.

The Promotion of Global Welfare

Fourth and finally, the United States, in seeking primacy, has
been willing to use its power not only to advance its interests
but to promote the welfare of people all over the globe. The
United States is the earth's leading source of positive externali-
ties for the world. The U.S. military has participated in over
fifty operations since the end of the Cold War—and most of
those missions have been humanitarian in nature. Indeed, the

U.S. military is the earth's "911 force"—it serves, *de facto*, as the world's police, the global paramedic and the planet's fire department. Whenever there is a natural disaster, earthquake, flood, drought, volcanic eruption, typhoon or tsunami, the United States assists the countries in need. On the day after Christmas in 2004, a tremendous earthquake and tsunami occurred in the Indian Ocean near Sumatra, killing some 300,000 people. The United States was the first to respond with aid. Washington followed up with a large contribution of aid and deployed the U.S. military to South and Southeast Asia for many months to help with the aftermath of the disaster. About 20,000 U.S. soldiers, sailors, airmen and marines responded by providing water, food, medical aid, disease treatment and prevention as well as forensic assistance to help identify the bodies of those killed. Only the U.S. military could have accomplished this Herculean effort. No other force possesses the communications capabilities or global logistical reach of the U.S. military. In fact, UN peacekeeping operations depend on the United States to supply UN forces.

American generosity has done more to help the United States fight the War on Terror than almost any other measure. Before the tsunami, 80 percent of Indonesian public opinion was opposed to the United States; after it, 80 percent had a favorable opinion of America. Two years after the disaster, and in poll after poll, Indonesians still have overwhelmingly positive views of the United States. In October 2005, an enormous earthquake struck Kashmir, killing about 74,000 people and leaving three million homeless. The U.S. military responded immediately, diverting helicopters fighting the War on Terror in nearby Afghanistan to bring relief as soon as possible. To help those in need, the United States also provided financial aid to Pakistan; and, as one might expect from those witnessing the munificence of the United States, it left a lasting impression about America. For the first time since 9/11, polls of Pakistani opinion have found that more people are favorable toward the United States than unfavorable, while support for Al-Qaeda dropped to its lowest level. Whether in Indonesia or Kashmir, the money was well-spent because it helped people in the wake of disasters, but it also had a real impact on the War on Terror. When people in the Muslim world witness the U.S. military conducting a humanitarian mission, there is a clearly positive impact on Muslim opinion of the United States. As the War on Terror is a war of ideas and opinion as much as military action, for the United States humanitarian missions are the equivalent of a blitzkrieg.

The Need for U.S. Primacy

There is no other state, group of states or international organization that can provide these global benefits. None even comes close. The United Nations cannot because it is riven with conflicts and major cleavages that divide the international body time and again on matters great and trivial. Thus it lacks the ability to speak with one voice on salient issues and to act as a unified force once a decision is reached. The EU [European Union] has similar problems. Does anyone expect Russia or China to take up these responsibilities? They may have the desire, but they do not have the capabilities. Let's face it: for the time being, American primacy remains humanity's only practical hope of solving the world's ills.

While the benefits of American primacy are considerable, no country can ever escape from the iron law of Economics 101—there is no free lunch. American primacy is no exception. Leadership requires that the United States incur costs and run risks not borne by other countries. These costs can be stark and brutal, and they have to be faced directly by proponents of primacy. It means that some Americans will die in the service of their country. These are the costs, and they are significant. Americans should be conscious of them and use them in their contemplation of the value of primacy. Additionally, the costs of primacy must impose upon American policy makers a sharp focus and prudence concerning how they wield American power. Equally, all Americans should be aware of the benefits that flow from primacy and that they enjoy.

While primacy's advantages and costs must be weighed objectively and solemnly, the scholars who are proclaiming that the sky is falling, primacy is doomed and America must retrench have to confront the reality of U.S. power. The world is a long way from seeing the end of American primacy, and it is in America's interest—and the world's—to have it last as long as possible.

3

The U.S. Military Presence Around the World Needs to End

Chalmers Johnson

In the following viewpoint Chalmers Johnson argues that the United States needs to liquidate its military empire by closing foreign military bases, bringing troops home, and selling base assets. Johnson claims that there are three reasons for liquidation. First, U.S. military spending is going to bankrupt the country. Second, the war in Afghanistan is a losing battle. Finally, the culture of the military abroad has led to a crisis of sexual violence. He concludes with a ten-step proposal to liquidate the U.S. empire. Johnson is president of the Japan Policy Research Institute and author of a trilogy about American military power: Blowback: The Costs and Consequences of American Empire; The Sorrows of Empire: Militarism, Secrecy, and the End of the Republic; *and* Nemesis: The Last Days of the American Republic.

However ambitious President Barack Obama's domestic plans, one unacknowledged issue has the potential to destroy any reform efforts he might launch. Think of it as the 800-pound gorilla in the American living room: our longstanding reliance on imperialism and militarism in our relations with other countries and the vast, potentially ruinous global empire of bases that goes with it. The failure to begin to deal with our bloated military establishment and the profligate use of it in missions for which it is hopelessly inappropriate will, sooner rather than later, condemn the United States to a devastating trio of consequences: imperial overstretch, perpetual war and insolvency, leading to a likely collapse similar to that of the former Soviet Union.

A Bloated Empire

According to the 2008 official Pentagon inventory of our military bases around the world, our empire consists of 865 facilities in more than forty countries and overseas US territories. We deploy over 190,000 troops in forty-six countries and territories. In just one such country, Japan, at the end of March 2008, we still had 99,295 people connected to US military forces living and working there—49,364 members of our armed services, 45,753 dependent family members, and 4,178 civilian employees. Some 13,975 of these were crowded into the small island of Okinawa, the largest concentration of foreign troops anywhere in Japan.

These massive concentrations of American military power outside the United States are not needed for our defense. They are, if anything, a prime contributor to our numerous conflicts with other countries. They are also unimaginably expensive. According to Anita Dancs, an analyst for the website Foreign Policy in Focus, the United States spends approximately $250 billion each year maintaining its global military presence. The sole purpose of this is to give us hegemony—that is, control or dominance—over as many nations on the planet as possible.

We are like the British at the end of World War II: desperately trying to shore up an empire that we never needed and can no longer afford, using methods that often resemble those of failed empires of the past—including the Axis powers of World War II and the former Soviet Union. There is an important lesson for us in the British decision, starting in 1945, to liquidate their empire relatively voluntarily, rather than being forced to do so by defeat in war, as were Japan and Germany, or by debilitating colonial conflicts, as were the French and Dutch. We should follow the British example. (Alas, they are currently backsliding and following our example by assisting us in the war in Afghanistan.)

Here are three basic reasons why we must liquidate our empire or else watch it liquidate us.

An Impending Economic Disaster

Shortly after his election as president, Barack Obama, in a speech announcing several members of his new cabinet, stated as fact that "[w]e have to maintain the strongest military on the planet." A few weeks later, on March 12, 2009, in a speech at the National Defense University in Washington, DC, the president again insisted, "Now make no mistake, this nation will maintain our military dominance. We will have the strongest armed forces in the history of the world." And in a commencement address to the cadets of the US Naval Academy on May 22, Obama stressed that "[w]e will maintain America's military dominance and keep you the finest fighting force the world has ever seen."

What he failed to note is that the United States no longer has the capability to remain a global hegemony, and to pretend otherwise is to invite disaster.

According to a growing consensus of economists and political scientists around the world, it is impossible for the United States to continue in that role while emerging into full view as a crippled economic power. No such configuration has ever persisted in the history of imperialism. The University of Chicago's Robert Pape, author of the important study *Dying to Win: The Strategic Logic of Suicide Terrorism*, typically writes:

America is in unprecedented decline. The self-inflicted wounds of the Iraq war, growing government debt, increasingly negative current-account balances and other internal economic weaknesses have cost the United States real power in today's world of rapidly spreading knowledge and technology. If present trends continue, we will look back on the Bush years as the death knell of American hegemony.

There is something absurd, even Kafkaesque, about our military empire. Jay Barr, a bankruptcy attorney, makes this point using an insightful analogy:

> Whether liquidating or reorganizing, a debtor who desires bankruptcy protection must provide a list of expenses, which, if considered reasonable, are offset against income to show that only limited funds are available to repay the bankrupted creditors. Now imagine a person filing for bankruptcy claiming that he could not repay his debts because he had the astronomical expense of maintaining at least 737 facilities overseas that provide exactly zero return on the significant investment required to sustain them. . . . He could not qualify for liquidation without turning over many of his assets for the benefit of creditors, including the valuable foreign real estate on which he placed his bases.

In other words, the United States is not seriously contemplating its own bankruptcy. It is instead ignoring the meaning of its precipitate economic decline and flirting with insolvency.

Nick Turse, author of *The Complex: How the Military Invades Our Everyday Lives*, calculates that we could clear $2.6 billion if we would sell our base assets at Diego Garcia in the Indian Ocean and earn another $2.2 billion if we did the same with Guantánamo Bay in Cuba. These are only two of our more than 800 overblown military enclaves.

Our unwillingness to retrench, no less liquidate, represents a striking historical failure of the imagination. In his first official visit to China since becoming Treasury Secretary, Timothy Geithner assured an audience of students at Beijing University,

"Chinese assets [invested in the United States] are very safe." According to press reports, the students responded with loud laughter. Well they might.

In May 2009, the Office of Management and Budget predicted that in 2010 the United States will be burdened with a budget deficit of at least $1.75 trillion. This includes neither a projected $640 billion budget for the Pentagon, nor the costs of waging two remarkably expensive wars. The sum is so immense that it will take several generations for American citizens to repay the costs of George W. Bush's imperial adventures—if they ever can or will. It represents about 13 percent of our current gross domestic product (that is, the value of everything we produce). It is worth noting that the target demanded of European nations wanting to join the Euro Zone is a deficit no greater than 3 percent of GDP.

Thus far, President Obama has announced measly cuts of only $8.8 billion in wasteful and worthless weapons spending, including his cancellation of the F-22 fighter aircraft. The actual Pentagon budget for next year [2010] will, in fact, be larger, not smaller, than the bloated final budget of the Bush era. Far bolder cuts in our military expenditures will obviously be required in the very near future if we intend to maintain any semblance of fiscal integrity.

The Failing War in Afghanistan

One of our major strategic blunders in Afghanistan was not to have recognized that both Great Britain and the Soviet Union attempted to pacify Afghanistan using the same military methods as ours and failed disastrously. We seem to have learned nothing from Afghanistan's modern history—to the extent that we even know what it is. Between 1849 and 1947, Britain sent almost annual expeditions against the Pashtun tribes and sub-tribes living in what was then called the North-West Frontier Territories—the area along either side of the artificial border between Afghanistan and Pakistan called the

Durand Line. This frontier was created in 1893 by Britain's foreign secretary for India, Sir Mortimer Durand.

Neither Britain nor Pakistan has ever managed to establish effective control over the area. As the eminent historian Louis Dupree put it in his book *Afghanistan*: "Pashtun tribes, almost genetically expert at guerrilla warfare after resisting centuries of all comers and fighting among themselves when no comers were available, plagued attempts to extend the Pax Britannica into their mountain homeland." An estimated 41 million Pashtuns live in an undemarcated area along the Durand Line and profess no loyalties to the central governments of either Pakistan or Afghanistan. . . .

Obama's mid-2009 "surge" of troops into southern Afghanistan and particularly into Helmand Province, a Taliban stronghold, is fast becoming darkly reminiscent of General William Westmoreland's continuous requests in Vietnam for more troops and his promises that if we would ratchet up the violence just a little more and tolerate a few more casualties, we would certainly break the will of the Vietnamese insurgents. This was a total misreading of the nature of the conflict in Vietnam, just as it is in Afghanistan today.

Twenty years after the forces of the Red Army withdrew from Afghanistan in disgrace, the last Russian general to command them, Gen. Boris Gromov, issued his own prediction: Disaster, he insisted, will come to the thousands of new forces Obama is sending there, just as it did to the Soviet Union's, which lost some 15,000 soldiers in its own Afghan war. We should recognize that we are wasting time, lives and resources in an area where we have never understood the political dynamics and continue to make the wrong choices.

Sexual Violence at Overseas Bases

In March [2009], *New York Times* op-ed columnist Bob Herbert noted, "Rape and other forms of sexual assault against women is the great shame of the US armed forces, and there is no evidence that this ghastly problem, kept out of sight as much as possible, is diminishing." He continued:

> New data released by the Pentagon showed an almost 9 percent increase in the number of sexual assaults—2,923—and a 25 percent increase in such assaults reported by women serving in Iraq and Afghanistan [over the past year]. Try to imagine how bizarre it is that women in American uniforms who are enduring all the stresses related to serving in a combat zone have to also worry about defending themselves against rapists wearing the same uniform and lining up in formation right beside them.

The problem is exacerbated by having our troops garrisoned in overseas bases located cheek-by-jowl next to civilian populations and often preying on them like foreign conquerors. For example, sexual violence against women and girls by American GIs has been out of control in Okinawa, Japan's poorest prefecture, ever since it was permanently occupied by our soldiers, Marines, and airmen some sixty-four years ago.

That island was the scene of the largest anti-American demonstrations since the end of World War II after the 1995 kidnapping, rape and attempted murder of a 12-year-old schoolgirl by two Marines and a sailor. The problem of rape has been ubiquitous around all of our bases on every continent and has probably contributed as much to our being loathed abroad as the policies of the Bush administration or our economic exploitation of poverty-stricken countries whose raw materials we covet.

The Problem with SOFAs

The military itself has done next to nothing to protect its own female soldiers or to defend the rights of innocent bystanders forced to live next to our often racially biased and predatory troops. "The military's record of prosecuting rapists is not just lousy, it's atrocious," writes Herbert. In territories occupied by American military forces, the high command and the State

Department make strenuous efforts to enact so-called "Status of Forces Agreements" (SOFAs) that will prevent host governments from gaining jurisdiction over our troops who commit crimes overseas. The SOFAs also make it easier for our military to spirit culprits out of a country before they can be apprehended by local authorities.

This issue was well illustrated by the case of an Australian teacher, a long-time resident of Japan, who in April 2002 was raped by a sailor from the aircraft carrier USS *Kitty Hawk*, then based at the big naval base at Yokosuka. She identified her assailant and reported him to both Japanese and US authorities. Instead of his being arrested and effectively prosecuted, the victim herself was harassed and humiliated by the local Japanese police. Meanwhile, the US discharged the suspect from the Navy but allowed him to escape Japanese law by returning him to the US, where he lives today.

In the course of trying to obtain justice, the Australian teacher discovered that almost fifty years earlier, in October 1953, the Japanese and American governments signed a secret "understanding" as part of their SOFA in which Japan agreed to waive its jurisdiction if the crime was not of "national importance to Japan." The US argued strenuously for this codicil because it feared that otherwise it would face the likelihood of some 350 servicemen per year being sent to Japanese jails for sex crimes.

Since that time the US has negotiated similar wording in SOFAs with Canada, Ireland, Italy and Denmark. According to the *Handbook of the Law of Visiting Forces* (2001), the Japanese practice has become the norm for SOFAs throughout the world, with predictable results. In Japan, of 3,184 US military personnel who committed crimes between 2001 and 2008, 83 percent were not prosecuted. In Iraq, we have just signed a SOFA that bears a strong resemblance to the first postwar one we had with Japan: namely, military personnel and military contractors accused of off-duty crimes will remain in US custody while Iraqis investigate. This is, of course, a perfect opportunity to spirit the culprits out of the country before they can be charged.

A Better Solution

Within the military itself, the journalist Dahr Jamail, author of *Beyond the Green Zone: Dispatches from an Unembedded Journalist in Occupied Iraq*, speaks of the "culture of unpunished sexual assaults" and the "shockingly low numbers of courts martial" for rapes and other forms of sexual attacks. Helen Benedict, author of *The Lonely Soldier: The Private War of Women Serving in Iraq*, quotes this figure in a 2009 Pentagon report on military sexual assaults: 90 percent of the rapes in the military are never reported at all and, when they are, the consequences for the perpetrator are negligible.

It is fair to say that the US military has created a worldwide sexual playground for its personnel and protected them to a large extent from the consequences of their behavior. As a result a group of female veterans in 2006 created the Service Women's Action Network (SWAN). Its agenda is to spread the word that "no woman should join the military."

I believe a better solution would be to radically reduce the size of our standing army, and bring the troops home from countries where they do not understand their environments and have been taught to think of the inhabitants as inferior to themselves.

Ten Steps Toward Liquidating the Empire

Dismantling the American empire would, of course, involve many steps. Here are ten key places to begin:

1. We need to put a halt to the serious environmental damage done by our bases planet-wide. We also need to stop writing SOFAs that exempt us from any responsibility for cleaning up after ourselves.

2. Liquidating the empire will end the burden of carrying our empire of bases and so of the "opportunity costs" that go with them—the things we might otherwise do with our talents and resources but can't or won't.

3. As we already know (but often forget), imperialism breeds the use of torture. In the 1960s and 1970s we helped overthrow the elected governments in Brazil and Chile and underwrote regimes of torture that prefigured our own treatment of prisoners in Iraq and Afghanistan. Dismantling the empire would potentially mean a real end to the modern American record of using torture abroad.

4. We need to cut the ever-lengthening train of camp followers, dependents, civilian employees of the Department of Defense and hucksters—along with their expensive medical facilities, housing requirements, swimming pools, clubs, golf courses and so forth—that follow our military enclaves around the world.

5. We need to discredit the myth promoted by the military-industrial complex that our military establishment is valuable

to us in terms of jobs, scientific research, and defense. These alleged advantages have long been discredited by serious economic research. Ending empire would make this happen.

6. As a self-respecting democratic nation, we need to stop being the world's largest exporter of arms and munitions and quit educating Third World militaries in the techniques of torture, military coups, and service as proxies for our imperialism. A prime candidate for immediate closure is the so-called School of the Americas, the US Army's infamous military academy at Fort Benning, Georgia, for Latin American military officers.

7. Given the growing constraints on the federal budget, we should abolish the Reserve Officers' Training Corps and other long-standing programs that promote militarism in our schools.

8. We need to restore discipline and accountability in our armed forces by radically scaling back our reliance on civilian contractors, private military companies and agents working for the military outside the chain of command and the Uniform Code of Military Justice. Ending empire would make this possible.

9. We need to reduce, not increase, the size of our standing army and deal much more effectively with the wounds our soldiers receive and combat stress they undergo.

10. To repeat the main message of this essay, we must give up our inappropriate reliance on military force as the chief means of attempting to achieve foreign policy objectives.

Unfortunately, few empires of the past voluntarily gave up their dominions in order to remain independent, self-governing polities. The two most important recent examples are the British and Soviet empires. If we do not learn from their examples, our decline and fall is foreordained.

4

All Foreign U.S. Military Bases Should Be Closed

Joseph Gerson

In the following viewpoint Joseph Gerson gives ten reasons why the United States should withdraw all foreign military bases. He contends that the existence of foreign military bases increases the likelihood of war. Additionally, he claims that these bases harm foreign nations by undermining their sovereignty, preventing democracy, and seizing property. Gerson argues that U.S. troops abroad cause many problems in host nations, and the bases cause environmental damage and damage to local people. Gerson is director of programs and director of the Peace and Economic Security Program for the American Friends Service Committee. He is the author of Empire and the Bomb.

*B*ases increase the likelihood of war. The US maintains an unprecedented infrastructure of more than 700 US foreign military bases. In recent years such bases have been essential to the US wars against Iraq, the 1998 war against Serbia, the US invasion of Panama, and the current wars within Colombia and the Philippines. The 200-plus US military bases and installations in Japan and South Korea increase the likelihood of future US wars against North Korea and China.

Bases provide a launching point for nuclear attack. In many ways, the US first-strike nuclear doctrine is made possible by the forward deployment of nuclear weapons in Belgium, Britain, Greece, Germany, Holland, and Turkey. US communica-

Joseph Gerson, "10 Reasons to Withdraw U.S. Foreign Military Bases," *Peacework*, vol. 34, February 2007, pp. 16–17. Reproduced by permission.

tions bases in Britain, Japan, Australia, and other nations are essential for communicating orders to initiate nuclear war and for targeting nuclear and other high-tech weapons.

The Harms to Foreign Nations

Bases undermine the sovereignty of nations. Hawai'i, the Philippines, Guam, Puerto Rico, and Cuba were invaded and occupied by the US because they were ideal sites for bases needed to conquer markets in China, elsewhere in Asia, and Latin America. Colonial and client governments were imposed or created by the US to ensure continued US access to the bases. After the wars in which they were defeated, the US has insisted that Japan, Germany, Serbia and other nations "host" US military bases for the long term. Consistent with this tradition, the [George W.] Bush administration is spending $1 billion a year for "enduring" military bases in Iraq.

Bases hurt democracy and human rights. The US has supported or imposed dictators and other repressive governments to gain or preserve access to military bases. For more than a decade, Presidents [Richard] Nixon, [Gerald] Ford, [Jimmy] Carter, and [Ronald] Reagan supported the brutal [Ferdinand] Marcos dictatorship in the Philippines to preserve the US hold on strategically located air and naval bases. In Saudi Arabia and Kuwait, the US has defended repressive monarchies to secure its military bases as well as privileged access to oil reserves. The presence of US military bases contributes to the cultural genocide of indigenous peoples in Hawai'i and Guam.

Many bases are built on seized property. The recent bulldozing of Daechuri village in South Korea to make way for a new US military headquarters while inhabitants protested was not unique. Military bases are often built on seized private property, on land which the host nation forces its citizens to "rent" to the US, or on communal property. The most extreme case is Diego Garcia. There, to make way for two mile-

According to Gerson, U.S. military bases in foreign countries, like the one pictured in Guantánamo Bay, Cuba, increase the likelihood of war. AP Images.

long runways, a massive naval port, and pre-positioned US weapons, *all* of the island's people were deported.

Problems Caused by U.S. Troops

Bases are a source of sexual violence. The use of communities near bases for "Rest and Relaxation" makes local children and women, especially sex workers, vulnerable to sexual harassment, rape, beatings, and murder. Levels of sexual violence can be a function of the relative power of host nations. Last year [2006] Marines involved in the rape of a Filipina were shielded by provisions of the Visiting Forces Agreement in the Philippines. In contrast, comparable agreements between the US and oil-rich Gulf states have at least partly shielded local women from sexual aggression by US troops.

Off-duty troops commit many crimes. Most GIs are law-abiding, but many alienated and drunken troops do commit a disproportionate number of crimes. Worse, they are often protected by the provisions of unequal treaties which give the

US military "primary right to exercise jurisdiction over members of the US armed forces." In Korea, a deep wound was the killing of two schoolgirls who were run over by a US tank; no-one was held accountable. This year in the Philippines, after a US Marine was convicted of rape in a Philippines court, the US exerted diplomatic pressure at the highest level to effect his removal, during the appeal process, to the US Embassy (rather than the Philippines jail to which the judge had consigned him).

The Damage Done to People and Environments

Bases cause environmental damage. In 2000, US Secretary of State Madeleine Albright conceded the legacy of "serious public and environmental problems" caused by US military bases in the Philippines but she reiterated that the US has no legal obligation to clean up the deadly residue. The US Defense Department has identified at least 70 military sites in Europe where its bases have caused serious environmental damage. In one egregious case, the US military was caught disposing of deadly formaldehyde directly into the Han River which runs through Seoul, South Korea.

Bases bring the risk of life-threatening accidents. Military accidents can kill and injure people. The most dangerous accidents involve nuclear weapons. An attack aircraft rolled off the US aircraft carrier *Ticonderoga* 80 miles off the coast of Okinawa, embedding its hydrogen bomb in the sea bed two miles below. More common are accidents like the Marine pilot whose low-flying jet severed a ski lift cable in Italy, killing 20 people; bombs that missed their practice targets, killing a civilian in Vieques, Puerto Rico and destroying homes in the Korean village of Maehyangri; and the stray bullets and shells used in live-fire exercises that strike people's homes and property in Kin Town, Okinawa.

Military spending jeopardizes human needs and opportunities. The Pentagon squanders tens of billions of dollars on foreign military bases. In addition to war-fighting capabilities, expenses include housing for families of US warriors, commissaries where US troops and their families enjoy special discounts, and pristine golf courses. Meanwhile, human needs of both US and host nation people go unmet. In Japan and other host nations, anger is building as their tax dollars are used to help pay for the intrusive military bases and their luxury accommodations, while local people go without adequate housing and social services.

5

U.S. Military Occupations Abroad Inspire Resentment in Occupied Nations

Stephen M. Walt

In the following viewpoint Stephen Walt contends that Americans do not fully appreciate why there is so much resistance to U.S. military occupation in foreign nations. He argues that the experience of living in an occupied country is humiliating and disruptive, causing some people to strike out against the occupier. Walt uses the example of Reconstruction after the U.S. Civil War to illustrate how an occupied nation—in this case, the South— might react to being occupied. He concludes that U.S. occupations should be avoided because of the potential for enduring hatred and resentment toward the United States. Walt is the Robert and Renee Belfer Professor of International Affairs at Harvard University's John F. Kennedy School of Government and author of Taming American Power: The Global Response to U.S. Primacy.

One of the many barriers to developing a saner U.S. foreign policy is our collective failure to appreciate why military occupations generate so much hatred, resentment, and resistance, and why we should therefore go to enormous lengths to avoid getting mired in them. Costly occupations are an activity you hope your adversaries undertake, especially in areas of little intrinsic strategic value. We blundered into Somalia in the early 1990s without realizing that we weren't wel-

Stephen M. Walt, "Why They Hate Us (I): On Military Occupation," *Foreign Policy*, November 23, 2009. Reproduced by permission.

come; we invaded Iraq thinking we would be greeted as liberators, and we still don't fully understand why many Afghans resent our presence and why some are driven to take up arms against us.

The Resistance to Foreign Occupation

The American experience is hardly unique: Britain's occupation of Iraq after World War I triggered fierce opposition, and British forces in Mandate Palestine eventually faced armed resistance from both Arab and Zionist groups. French rule in Algeria, Syria, Lebanon, and Indochina spawned several violent resistance movements, and Russia has fought Chechen insurgents in the 19th, 20th and 21st centuries. The Shiite population of southern Lebanon initially welcomed Israel's invasion in 1982, but the IDF [Israel Defense Forces] behaved badly and stayed too long, which led directly to the formation of *Hezbollah* [Islamist resistance movement]. Israelis were also surprised by the first intifida [uprising] in 1987, having mistakenly assumed that their occupation of the West Bank was benevolent and that the Palestinians there would be content to be governed by the IDF forever.

Military occupation generates resistance because it is humiliating, disruptive, arbitrary and sometimes terrifying to its objects, even when the occupying power is acting from more-or-less benevolent motives. If you've ever been caught in a speed trap by a rude or abusive policeman (I have), or selected out for special attention crossing a border (ditto), you have a mild sense of what this is like. You are at the mercy of the person in charge, who is inevitably well-armed and can do pretty much whatever he (or she) wants. Any sign of protest will only make things go badly—and in some situations will get you arrested, beaten, or worse—so you choke down your anger and just put up with it. Now imagine that this is occurring after you've waited for hours at some internal checkpoint, that none of the occupiers speak your language, and that it is

Extended U.S. military occupations should be avoided because they often lead to resentment and hatred toward the United States. AP Images.

like this *every single day*. And occasionally the occupying power kills innocent people by mistake, engages in other forms of indiscriminate force, and does so with scant regard for local customs and sensibilities. Maintain this situation long enough, and some members of the local population will start looking for ways to strike back. Some of them may even decide to strap on explosive vests or get behind the wheel of a explosives-laden truck, and sacrifice themselves.

An Analogy with the Civil War

It is sometimes said that Americans don't understand this phenomenon because the United States has never been conquered and occupied. But this simply isn't true. After the Civil War, a "foreign army" occupied the former Confederacy and imposed a new political order that most white southerners found abhorrent. The first Reconstruction Act of 1867 put most southern states under formal military control, supervised the writing of new state constitutions, and sought to enfranchise and empower former slaves. It also attempted to rebuild the south economically, but the reconstruction effort was undermined by corruption and poor administration. Sound familiar? However laudable the aims may have been, the results were precisely what one would expect. Northern occupation eventually triggered violent resistance by the Ku Klux Klan, White League, Red Shirts, and other insurgent groups, which helped thwart Reconstruction and paved the way for the Jim Crow system that lasted until the second half of the 20th century.

Nor should we forget how long a profound sense of anger and resentment lasted. I was recently discussing this issue with a distinguished American journalist who grew up in the South, and he told me that one hundred years after the end of the Civil War, he was still being taught songs that expressed a lingering hatred of what the Yankees had done. Here are a couple of stanzas from one of them—"I'm a Good Old Rebel"—written by a former Confederate officer and first published in 1914:

I hates the Yankee nation, and ev-
erything they do,
I hates the Declaration of Indepen-
dence too.
I hates the glorious Union, 'tis
dripping with our blood
I hates their striped banner, I
fought it all I could.
Three hundred thousand Yankees
lie stiff in Southern dust;
We got three hundred thousand,
before they conquered us
They died of Southern fever, and
Southern steel and shot,
I wish they was three million, in-
stead of what we got.

Or to take a more recent (1974), less poetic example, from Lynyrd Skynyrd:

> Well I heard Mr. Young sing about
> her,
> Well I heard old Neil put her
> down.
> Well, I hope Neil Young will re-
> member,
> A Southern man don't need him
> around anyhow.

An Enduring Source of Resentment

This is what defeat in war and prolonged occupation does to a society: it generates hatred and resentment that can last a century or more. Hatred of the "party of Lincoln" kept the South solidly Democratic for decades, and its political character remains distinctly different even today, nearly 150 years after the civil war ended. (Among other things, Barack Obama has favorable job approval ratings in every region of the country except the South). And don't forget that unlike our current presence in Iraq and Afghanistan, the occupying forces of the North spoke the same language and had been part of the same country prior to the war, in some cases, there were even strong family connections on both sides of the Mason-Dixon line. Yet defeat in war and military occupation were an enduring source of division for many years thereafter.

The bottom line is that you don't need to be a sociologist, political scientist, or a student of colonialism or foreign cultures to understand why military occupation is such a poisonous activity and why it usually fails. If you're an American, you just need to read a bit about Reconstruction and reflect on how its effects—along with the effects of slavery itself—have persisted across generations. If that's not enough, visit a society that is currently experiencing occupation, and take the time to go through a checkpoint or two. Then you might understand why the local population doesn't view the occupying forces as benevolent and isn't as grateful as occupiers often think they ought to be.

6

The U.S. Military Presence in Iraq Must Continue

Thomas E. Ricks

In the following viewpoint Thomas Ricks contends that 2010 marks a turning point in the war in Iraq. He argues that the plan to remove most troops by September and all troops by the end of 2011 is not warranted given the lack of a political breakthrough in Iraq. Ricks worries that if all troops are removed on schedule, a civil war will follow. To avoid this, he concludes that it is necessary to have a continued U.S. military presence in Iraq for years to come. Ricks is a senior fellow at the Center for New American Security—a defense policy think tank—and author of The Gamble: General David Petraeus and the American Military Adventure in Iraq, 2006–2008.

Iraq's March 7 [2010] national election, and the formation of a new government that will follow, carry huge implications for both Iraqis and American policy. It appears now that the results are unlikely to resolve key political struggles that could return the country to sectarianism and violence.

If so, President [Barack] Obama may find himself later this year considering whether once again to break his campaign promises about ending the war, and to offer to keep tens of thousands of troops in Iraq for several more years. Surprisingly, that probably is the best course for him, and for Iraqi leaders, to pursue.

A Turning Point in Iraq

Whether or not the elections bring the long-awaited political breakthrough that genuinely ends the fighting there, 2010 is likely to be a turning-point year in the war, akin to the summer of 2003 (when the United States realized that it faced an insurgency) and 2006 (when that insurgency morphed into a small but vicious civil war and American policy came to a dead end). For good or ill, this is likely the year we will begin to see the broad outlines of post-occupation Iraq. . . .

The political situation is far less certain, and I think less stable, than most Americans believe. A retired Marine colonel I know, Gary Anderson, just returned from Iraq and predicts a civil war or military coup by September. Another friend, the journalist Nir Rosen, avers that Iraq is on a long-term peaceful course. Both men know Iraq well, having spent years working there. I have not seen such a wide discrepancy in expert views since late 2005.

The period surrounding the surge of 2007 has been misremembered. It was not about simply sending 30,000 more troops to Iraq; it was about using force differently, moving the troops off big bases to work with Iraqi units and live among the people. Perhaps even more significantly, the surge signaled a change in American attitudes, with more humility about what could be done, more willingness to listen to Iraqis, and with quietly but sharply reduced ambitions.

The [George W.] Bush administration's grandiose original vision of transforming Iraq into a beacon of democracy that would alter the Middle East and drain the swamps of terrorism was scuttled and replaced by the more realistic goal of getting American forces out and leaving behind a country that was somewhat stable and, with luck, perhaps democratic and respectful of human rights. As part of the shift, the American commander, Gen. David Petraeus, also effectively put the Sunni insurgency on the American payroll.

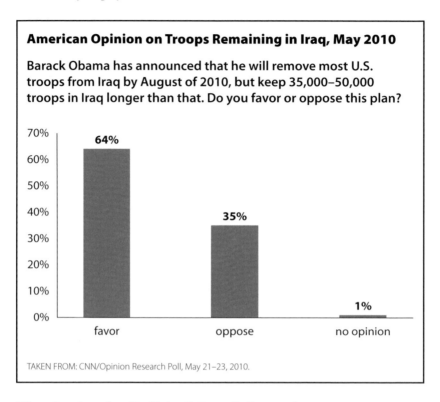

American Opinion on Troops Remaining in Iraq, May 2010

Barack Obama has announced that he will remove most U.S. troops from Iraq by August of 2010, but keep 35,000–50,000 troops in Iraq longer than that. Do you favor or oppose this plan?

TAKEN FROM: CNN/Opinion Research Poll, May 21–23, 2010.

The Lack of a Political Breakthrough

Looking back now, I think the surge was the right thing to do. In rejecting the view of the majority of his military advisers and embracing the course proposed by a handful of dissidents, President Bush found his finest moment. That said, the larger goal of the surge was to facilitate a political breakthrough, which has not happened.

All the existential questions that plagued Iraq before the surge remain unanswered. How will oil revenue be shared among the country's major groups? What is to be the fundamental relationship between Shiites, Sunnis and Kurds? Will Iraq have a strong central government or be a loose confederation? And what will be the role of Iran (for my money, the biggest winner in the Iraq war thus far)?

Unfortunately, all of these questions have led to violence in the past, and could again just as the Obama administration's timeline calls for troops to leave areas that are far from quiet. The plan this year is to pull out about 10,000 troops a month for five months, beginning in late spring. That will halve the American military presence, with the remainder (other than a "residual force" of unspecified size) scheduled to be withdrawn in 2011. The withdrawal plan was written on the assumption that the elections would be held late in 2009 or early in 2010. Under the plan, troop numbers would be kept level to ensure stability in a vulnerable period, especially if the Sunnis were to feel that the electoral process was unfair, or if they were not given a role in the new government commensurate with their success at the polls.

The Withdrawal of U.S. Troops

But given the changed timetable, just as Iraqi political leaders are struggling to form a new government, American military leaders will be distracted by the myriad tasks of supervising major troop movements. On top of that, the deeper the troop withdrawals go, the more potentially destabilizing they will be—because the first withdrawals will be made in areas that are considered more secure, or where Iraqi forces are deemed more reliable or evenhanded.

By June, American troops may be leaving areas that are far from quiet, and where new tensions may be brewing as a result of the elections. Once again, the United States would be rushing toward failure in Iraq, as it did so often under the Bush administration, trying to pass responsibility to Iraqi officials and institutions before they are ready for the task.

By late summer, the Obama administration could find itself in the uncomfortable position of reconsidering its vows to get out of combat in Iraq by August and to remove all troops by the end of next year. This will be politically difficult for the president, but he has shown admirable flexibility in his handling of Iraq. My impression is that the American people now wish they had never heard of Iraq, but understand just what a mess it is and are willing to give the president a surprising amount of leeway.

Extending the American military presence will be even more politically controversial in Iraq, and for that reason, it would be best to let Iraqi leaders make the first public move to re-open the status of forces agreement of 2008, which calls for American troops to be out of the country by the end of next year. But I think leaders in both countries may come to recognize that the best way to deter a return to civil war is to find a way to keep 30,000 to 50,000 United States service members in Iraq for many years to come.

A Continued U.S. Military Presence

These troops' missions would be far narrower than during the surge era; their primary goal would be to train and advise Iraqi security forces and to carry out counterterrorism missions. (It is actually hard to get below 30,000 and still have an effective force; many troops are needed for logistics, maintenance, medical, intelligence, communications and headquarters jobs, and additional infantry units are then needed to protect the people performing those tasks.)

Such a relatively small, tailored force would not be big enough to wage a war, but it might be enough to deter a new one from breaking out. An Iraqi civil war would likely be a three- or four-sided affair, with the Shiites breaking into pro- and anti-Iranian factions. It could also easily metastasize into a regional war. Neighboring powers like Turkey and Iran are already involved in Iraqi affairs, and the Sunni Arab states would be unlikely to stand by and watch a Shiite-dominated regime in Baghdad slaughter the Sunni minority. A regional war in the middle of the world's oil patch could shake the global economy to its foundations and make the current recession look mild.

In addition, a continued American military presence could help Iraq move forward politically. No one there particularly likes having the Americans around, but many groups seem to trust the Americans as honest brokers. And there would be a moral, humanitarian and political benefit: Having American soldiers accompany Iraqi units may improve the behavior of Iraqi forces, discouraging relapses to Saddam Hussein-era abuses, or the use of force for private ends and feuds. Advisers not only instruct Iraqi commanders, they also monitor them.

As a longtime critic of the American invasion of Iraq, I am not happy about advocating a continued military presence there. Yet, to echo the counterinsurgency expert David Kilcullen, just because you invade a country stupidly doesn't mean you should leave it stupidly. The best argument against keeping troops in Iraq is the one some American military officers make, which is that a civil war is inevitable, and that by staying all we are doing is postponing it. That may be so, but I don't think it is worth gambling to find out.

7

A Continued Military Presence in Iraq Is a Bad Idea

George Will

In the following viewpoint George Will argues that the United States should remove all troops from Iraq by the end of 2011 at the latest. Will contends that although the situation in Iraq is unstable, it is time for the United States to hand over responsibility for the country to the Iraqis. Will rejects arguments for a continued U.S. military presence in Iraq based on concern about a return to civil war, claiming that to stay for that reason is just to delay the inevitable sectarian violence that will follow when the United States does leave. Will is a columnist for the Washington Post *and* Newsweek.

Since U.S. troops withdrew from Iraq's cities [June 30, 2009], two months have passed, and so has the illusion that Iraq is smoothly transitioning to a normality free of sectarian violence. Recently, Gen. Ray Odierno, commander of U.S. troops there, "blanched" when asked if the war is "functionally over." According to *The Post*'s Greg Jaffe, Odierno said:

"There are still civilians being killed in Iraq. We still have people that are attempting to attack the new Iraqi order and the move towards democracy and a more open economy. So we still have some work to do."

No, *we* don't, even if, as Jaffe reports, the presence of 130,000 U.S. troops "serves as a check on Iraqi military and political leaders' baser and more sectarian instincts." After almost 6 1/2 years, and 4,327 American dead and 31,483 wounded, with a war spiraling downward in Afghanistan, it would be indefensible for the U.S. military—overextended and in need of materiel [equipment] repair and mental recuperation—to loiter in Iraq to improve the instincts of corrupt elites. If there is a worse use of the U.S. military than "nation-building," it is adult supervision and behavior modification of other peoples' politicians.

An Irrelevant Presence

More than 725 Iraqis have been killed by terrorism since the June 30 pullback of U.S. forces from the cities. All U.S. combat units are to be withdrawn from the country within a year. Up to 50,000 can remain as "advisers" to an Iraqi government that is ostentatious about its belief that the presence of U.S. forces is superfluous and obnoxious.

The advisers are to leave by the end of 2011, by which time the final two years of the U.S. military presence will have achieved . . . what? Already that presence is irrelevant to the rising chaos, which the Iraqi government can neither contain nor refrain from participating in: Security forces seem to have been involved in the recent robbery of a state-run bank in central Baghdad.

Post columnist David Ignatius correctly argues that "without the backstop of U.S. support," Iraq is "desperately vulnerable" to Iranian pressure. He also reports, however, that an Iraqi intelligence official says Prime Minister Nouri al-Maliki's links with Iran are so close that he "uses an Iranian jet with an Iranian crew for his official travel." Whenever U.S. forces leave, Iran will still be Iraq's neighbor.

Kenneth Pollack of the Brookings Institution, writing in the *National Interest*, notes that although rising Iraqi nationalism might help "heal the rifts between Sunni and Shia," it also

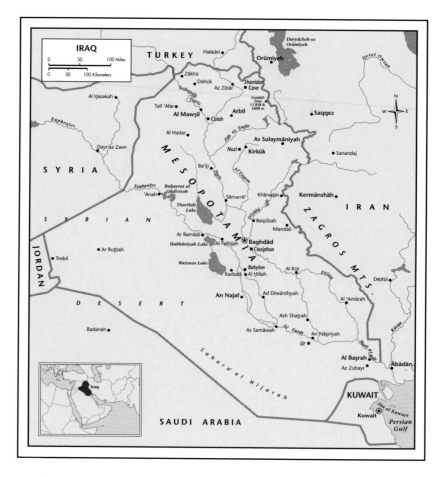

might exacerbate relations with the Kurdish semi-state in northern Iraq, where control of much oil and the city of Kirkuk is being contested.

The Withdrawal of U.S. Troops

The militia parties that ruled Iraq from 2003 to 2007 remain, Pollack says, the major political parties, although mostly without militias. They "still bribe and extort," "assassinate and kidnap," "steal and vandalize" and try to prevent the emergence of new political parties that are "more secular, more democratic, more representative, less corrupt and less violent." If they succeed and "America is forced out," Pollack says, "the glimmers of democracy will fade and Iraq will be lost again." But if democracy is still just a glimmer that will be extinguished by the withdrawal of a protective U.S. presence, its extinction can perhaps be delayed for two more years but cannot be prevented.

The 2008 U.S.-Iraq security agreement must be submitted to a referendum by *the* Iraqi people [not held as of July 2010]. If they reject it, U.S. forces must leave the country in a year. Pollack believes that if Maliki pushes to hold the referendum in January, coinciding with the national elections, the agreement will become the campaign issue and will indicate that Maliki wants U.S. forces removed in order to enlarge his freedom of action. The United States should treat this as a Dirty Harry Moment: Make our day.

Many scholars believe, Pollack says, that nations that suffer civil wars as large as Iraq's between 2004 and 2006 have "a terrifyingly high rate of recidivism." Two more years of U.S. military presence cannot control whether that is in Iraq's future. Some people believe the war in Iraq was not only "won," but vindicated by the success of the 2007 U.S. troop surge. Yet as Iraqi violence is resurgent, the logic of triumphalism leads here:

If, in spite of contrary evidence, the U.S. surge permanently dampened sectarian violence, *all* U.S. forces can come home sooner than the end of 2011. If, however, the surge did not so succeed, U.S. forces *must* come home sooner.

8

U.S. Military Intervention in the Middle East Leads to Hatred

Jacob Hornberger

In the following viewpoint Jacob Hornberger argues that the anger and rage felt by the Middle East toward the United States is a direct result of U.S. military intervention in that region. Hornberger claims that decades of intervention in Middle East politics, deadly economic sanctions toward Iraq, and the war of aggression in Iraq have all fueled the fire of hatred toward America. He concludes that the correct solution to end the rage and the associated terrorist acts against America is to end all overseas military intervention. Hornberger is founder and president of The Future of Freedom Foundation, an organization that works to advance freedom by promoting individual liberty, free markets, private property, and limited government.

When U.S. officials condemn the violence arising out of the anti-Mohammed cartoons published by the European press [in September 2005], they fail to recognize that the anger in the Middle East goes a lot deeper than the adverse reaction to the cartoons reflects.

For example, read the transcript of the federal court sentencing of Ramzi Yousef, the terrorist who attacked the World Trade Center in 1993. Whether you agree with anything he said is irrelevant. When you read the invective [insults] that he hurled at the judge just before his sentencing, you can

Jacob Hornberger, "Why They Hate Us," The Future of Freedom Foundation, February 13, 2006. Reproduced by permission.

reach but one conclusion: This is a very angry man. It is that same anger and rage that smoldered within many Middle Eastern men throughout the 1990s and into this century, culminating in the second terrorist attacks on the World Trade Center and on the Pentagon on 9/11.

Anger in the Middle East

No matter how angry Muslims become over the mocking of their religious symbols (i.e., the Koran and Mohammed), what U.S. officials would prefer to ignore is the depth of anger that Muslims also feel at having been subjected to the arrogant, pretentious, brutal, and humiliating conduct of U.S. government officials. In fact, one cannot help but wonder whether the anger that has built up within Middle Easterners as a consequence of U.S. governmental conduct in that part of the world has contributed to the enormous anti-Western reaction to the publishing of tasteless cartoons by a Danish newspaper.

After 9/11, many Americans had no idea why there was so much anger and rage in the Middle East, especially against the United States. All their lives, Americans had been taught that foreign policy was for federal "experts" and, thus, they had chosen not to concern themselves with what their federal officials were doing to people abroad. Innocently believing that federal overseas personnel, including the CIA [Central Intelligence Agency] and the military, had been helping foreigners for decades, Americans had no reason to doubt the official U.S. pronouncement immediately after 9/11: "We are innocent. The terrorists hate us for our freedom and values. That's why they have attacked us."

What Americans didn't realize is that federal officials were being disingenuous when they made that pronouncement. U.S. officials knew full-well that that their decades-old U.S. interventionist policies in the Middle East were at the bottom of the volcanic rage that people bore in that part of the world.

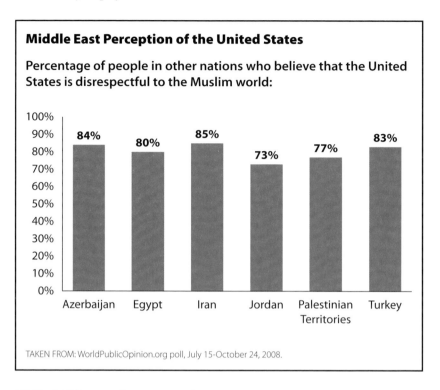

Middle East Perception of the United States

Percentage of people in other nations who believe that the United States is disrespectful to the Muslim world:

TAKEN FROM: WorldPublicOpinion.org poll, July 15-October 24, 2008.

U.S. Military Intervention

Consider:

1. The U.S. government's international paramilitary force, the CIA, covertly engineered the ouster of the popular and democratically elected prime minister of Iran and replaced him with a brutal dictator whose secret police tortured and terrorized the Iranian people for decades. Yet to this day, Americans cannot fathom why so many Iranians still hate the U.S. government.

2. The United States and other Western nations actively supported Saddam Hussein and his tyrannical regime, even delivering him the infamous weapons of mass destruction that U.S. officials later used as an excuse to invade Iraq.

3. In their role as imperial international policeman, U.S. officials turned on Saddam when he invaded Kuwait, even though the Iraqi invasion of Kuwait was no more the business

of the U.S. government than the U.S. invasion of Panama or Grenada was the business of Iraq. Moreover, the fact that U.S. officials had supported Saddam's attack on Iran and then later had turned a passive eye on his intention to attack Kuwait makes U.S. officials look even worse. Thousands of Iraqis were massacred and maimed by U.S. bombs and missiles in the Persian Gulf War, decimating Iraqi families.

4. After the Persian Gulf War, U.S. officials inspired Kurds and Shi'ites to rebel against Saddam and then stood aside as Saddam massacred them.

Deadly Economic Sanctions

5. Brutal economic sanctions were imposed on Iraq and then continued, year after year, for more than a decade, with the aim of forcing the Iraqi people to oust Saddam from power. The sanctions contributed to the deaths of hundreds of thousands of Iraqi children from disease and infection, especially from dirty water.

To this day, many Americans remain ignorant of the major role that the sanctions played in the smoldering anger and rage within the Middle East, culminating on 9/11. . . . High UN [United Nations] officials even resigned in protest at the genocide caused by the sanctions. Ramzi Yousef mentioned the deaths of the Iraqi children in his angry tirade to the judge.

Is it difficult to understand how Middle East anger turned into rage when UN Ambassador Madeleine Albright, expressing the callous mindset of her federal associates, told *60 Minutes* that the deaths of half a million Iraqi children from the sanctions were "worth it"?

A War of Aggression

6. There were the infamous no-fly zones over Iraq, by which U.S. officials continued killing Iraqis with bombs and missiles, even though the zones had never been authorized by either the UN or the U.S. Congress.

7. U.S. troops were knowingly and deliberately stationed on Islamic holy lands, in utter disregard for religious sensibilities of Muslims. In fact, is it not easier to understand the depth of the adverse Muslim reaction to the stationing of U.S. troops in those areas given the recent adverse reactions to U.S. military abuse of the Koran and to the publication of the cartoons mocking Mohammed? Does anyone honestly believe that U.S. officials were unaware of the potential for such adverse reaction when they stationed U.S. troops in those areas?

8. The U.S. government invaded and waged a war of aggression against Iraq under false and deceptive claims regarding weapons of mass destruction and then continued a brutal military occupation of the country under the deceptive rubric of "spreading democracy." The invasion and occupation have killed and maimed tens of thousands of innocent Iraqi people—innocent in the sense that neither they nor their government ever attacked the United States or even threatened to do so.

9. U.S. military and paramilitary forces tortured, sexually abused, raped, and murdered Iraqi men taken into custody. What better way to turn anger into rage than to knowingly and deliberately humiliate Iraqi men in such a manner rather than treat them like men and soldiers entitled to the protections of the Geneva convention [international agreement regarding treatment of prisoners of war], especially given that most of them were doing nothing worse than defending their nation against an illegal invasion and war of aggression by a foreign power?

10. The U.S. government has long provided unconditional financial and military support to the Israeli government as well as foreign aid to such pro-U.S. authoritarian regimes as Saudi Arabia, Jordan, and Egypt.

The Reason for the Anger

When someone is trying to kill you, it's of course important to defend yourself. But it's also important to try to figure out why he's trying to kill you. After all, if you're doing something wrong that has gotten him angry, then isn't it better to simply stop committing the wrongful act? In that case, his anger might dissipate, and he might even no longer want to kill you.

Today, there are Americans who cry, "It's too late. They already hate us and will always hate us and so we've got to keep killing them before they kill us."

But unless the entire Middle East is nuked, it is impossible to kill "all of them" because there will always be brothers, sisters, cousins, parents, children, grandchildren, or just friends of the dead who will seek vengeance.

Moreover, think about Vietnam. When the United States exited that country after killing more than a million Vietnamese, the Vietnamese communists left the United States alone. Today U.S. officials are even working with the Vietnamese communist regime to establish closer commercial ties.

The Right Solution

U.S. government meddling in the Middle East occurred long before 9/11 and, in fact, was the motivating cause for 9/11 (and the previous 1993 attack on the World Trade Center). Thus, U.S. officials have it all wrong—the solution is not to invade, bomb, kill, maim, and meddle even more. That will only exacerbate the anger and rage that engenders retaliatory terrorist attacks. Continuing the same policies that have produced volcanic anger and rage will only ensure more terrorism, more counterterrorism, more infringements on the freedom of the American people, and more increases in the Pentagon's budget.

The solution instead is for the American people to dismantle the U.S. government's overseas empire, requiring the federal government, especially the Pentagon, to withdraw from the Middle East (and the rest of the world) and also to liberate the American people to travel, trade, and interact freely with the people of the world (including both Vietnam and Cuba).

Dismantling the U.S. overseas empire would not, of course, end conflicts abroad but it would ensure that the U.S. government could not make matters worse, both for foreigners and Americans, with its meddling overseas interventions. The federal government's power would be limited to defending the United States from a foreign invasion, a virtually nonexistent threat at present, and to prosecuting criminal acts committed on American soil.

Equally important, by ending the federal government's isolation of the American people from the rest of the world, we not only would be restoring the constitutional republic our ancestors bequeathed to us, Americans also would once again have the opportunity to lead the world to freedom, peace, prosperity, and harmony.

9

The U.S. Military Presence in Afghanistan Must Continue

Michael Yon

In the following viewpoint Michael Yon argues that the United States needs to make a long-term commitment to Afghanistan in order to win the war and help the country succeed. He contends there is no easy solution to the situation in Afghanistan and a strictly counterterrorism approach is not enough. Yon proposes that the United States adopt Afghanistan for the long term, committing not only to a continued military presence, but also to improving education and infrastructure. Yon is a former Green Beret who has been reporting from Iraq and Afghanistan since 2004. He is the author of Moment of Truth in Iraq.

I respect the work of Dexter Filkins, who wrote this weekend's [October 14, 2009] *New York Times Magazine* story "Stanley McChrystal's Long War." Filkins is a seasoned war correspondent whose characterizations of Iraq ring true. Much of his latest piece resonates with my ongoing experiences in Afghanistan. Despite the great length of the article, the few points that did not resonate were more trivialities for discussion than disagreements. Filkins did a fine job.

To be clear, I have developed a strong belief that the war is winnable, though on current trends we will lose. Filkins seemed to present a similar argument. In my view, we need more troops and effort in Afghanistan—now—and our commitment must be intergenerational.

Michael Yon, "The War in Afghanistan Is Winnable," *National Review Online*, October 19, 2009. Reproduced by permission.

The Need for a Long-Term Commitment

In Filkins's article, a couple of seemingly small points are key-holes to profound realities, and to a few possible illusions. For instance, the idea that Afghans are tired of fighting seems wrong. Afghans often tell me they are tired of fighting, but those words are inconsistent with the bitter fact that the war intensifies with every change of season. The idea that Afghans are tired of war seems an illusion. *Some* Afghans are tired. I spend more time talking with older Afghans than with teenagers, and most of the older Afghans do seem weary. Yet according to the CIA [Central Intelligence Agency] World Factbook, the median age in Afghanistan is 17.6. The culture is old, but the population is a teenager. Most Afghans today probably had not reached puberty when al-Qaeda launched the 9/11 attacks. Eight years later, Afghanistan is more an illiterate kid than a country. The median age in the U.S. is 36.7. In addition to the tremendous societal disconnect between Americans and Afghans, there would be a generational gap even if those distant children were Americans.

We ask Afghans for help in defeating the enemies, yet the Afghans expect us to abandon them. Filkins pointed out that Afghans don't like to see Americans living in tents. Tents are for nomads. It would be foolish for Afghans in "Talibanastan" to cooperate with nomadic Americans only to be eviscerated by the Taliban when the nomads pack up. (How many times did we see similar things happen in Iraq?) The Afghans want to see us living in real buildings as a sign of permanency. The British forces at Sangin and associated bases live in temporary structures, as do the Americans at many of their bases. Our signals are clear. "If you are coming to stay," Afghans have told me in various ways, "build a real house. Build a real office. Don't live in tents."

A great many Iraqis wanted assurances that we would stay long enough to help their country survive but were not planning on making Iraq part of an American empire. It thus became important to convey signs of *semi*-permanence, signaling, "Yes, we will stay, and yes, we will leave." Conversely, Afghans in places like Helmand tend to have fond memories of Americans who came in the middle of last century, and those Afghans seem apt to cooperate. That much is clear. But Afghans need to sense our long-term commitment. They need to see houses made of stone, not tents and "Hescohabs" [temporary military structures].

Counterterrorism Is Not Enough

It's crucial to hold in constant memory that Afghanistan is the societal equivalent of an illiterate teenager. The child-nation will fail unless we are willing to adopt the people. Many Afghans clearly hope this will happen, though of course we have to phrase it slightly differently. Afghans are, after all, proud and xenophobic [wary of foreigners]. They are not just xeno-phobic but also Afghanophobic. Most houses are built like little Alamos.

Half-solutions failed in Iraq and are failing in Afghanistan. There will be no cheap, easy, or quick compromise that will lead to long-term success in Af-Pak [Afghanistan and Pakistan]. Adopting a scaled-back counterterrorism approach would be like dispatching the potent but tiny Delta Force to the Amazon jungles with orders to swat mosquitoes. We could give the Delta troops every Predator and Reaper [unmanned aerial vehicles] in our arsenal, yet 20 years from now they'd still be shooting Hellfire missiles at mosquitoes.

Gutting mid-level enemy leadership has been very effective in Iraq and Afghanistan, but only in a larger context. Using strictly a counterterrorism approach, we'll end up killing relatively zero mosquitoes—the Afghan birthrate alone will ensure that we never win—before coming down with war malaria. Counterterrorism in today's context remains important, but only as part of a broader strategy. Afghanistan was a special-operations playground for more than half a decade. Nobody can argue that our special-ops forces were not given plenty of assets and discretion. They also got more than a half-decade of free passes in the press. Gen. Stanley McChrystal is asking for more troops, not fewer. We need to provide him with the resources needed to win.[1]

Adoption for the Long Term

If Afghanistan is to succeed, we must adopt it. We must adopt an entire country, a troubled child, for many decades to come. We must show the Afghans that together we can severely damage the enemies, or bring them around, and together build a brighter future. The alternative is perpetual war and terrorism

1. McChrystal resigned from his commands in Afghanistan in June 2010 following un-flattering remarks made about Obama administration officials that were attributed to McChrystal.

American troops, like the ones pictured who are departing for Afghanistan, need to establish more permanence to give Afghans a sense of their long-term commitment. AP Images.

radiating from the biggest, possibly richest, and most war-prone drug dealers the world has ever seen. Under that scenario, Afghanistan could become the swamp that harbors the disease that eventually kills Pakistan, leaving its nuclear weapons on the table.

Adopting this child-nation means more than building up Afghan security forces. Afghanistan cannot finance its police and army, much less the education system and vast infrastructure needed to fashion and fuel a self-sustaining economy. Its uncontrolled population growth stems from ignorance. Only through the spread of education and opportunity can narcotics production, criminality, warlordism, and fanaticism be eroded.

Finally, while it is important to learn from the Soviet Union's successes and failures in Afghanistan, close comparisons between Coalition activities today and Soviet efforts in the 1980s quickly become silly. The Coalition can succeed where the Soviets failed. For that matter, we should also remember that the Soviets failed in the "easy" places where democracy now thrives, such as Lithuania, Poland, the Czech Republic, Hungary, and other countries that are now helping in Afghanistan, and where the U.S. is now welcome. I remember Poland, East Germany, Czechoslovakia, Romania, and others during the dark days. It is no wonder to me that the Soviets failed while freedom and democracy succeeded. People who saw Prague then and can see it today likely will have great difficulty explaining the differences to the uninitiated. The Coalition in Afghanistan is largely comprised of nations that have suffered greatly in recent times. They get it.

We should adopt Afghanistan for the long term. If not, there will be perpetual and growing trouble. We can succeed in Afghanistan where others failed.

10

The U.S. Military Presence in Afghanistan Should End

Erik Leaver

In the following viewpoint Erik Leaver contends that the United States needs an exit strategy from Afghanistan. He argues that little progress has been made during the last several years that the United States has been at war in Afghanistan. Leaver believes that neither additional troops nor a focus on counterterrorism could work without a never-ending U.S. military presence. He concludes that a timetable is needed for all U.S. troops to leave Afghanistan, and energy should be refocused on international support and economic development of the country. Leaver is the communications manager at the Institute for Policy Studies (IPS) in Washington, D.C.

For years, the war in Afghanistan has been in crisis. But now with a failed Afghan election, the resurgence of the Taliban as a political power, NATO [North Atlantic Treaty Organization] allies withdrawing from the battlefield, and Pakistan's tribal areas under increasing influence from the Taliban and al-Qaeda, the situation looks worse than ever. [U.S. president Barack] Obama and his team are spinning their wheels trying to devise a policy to right the sinking ship, but the most sensible solution, for Afghans and U.S. citizens, is to start planning a way out.

The Lack of Progress in Afghanistan

As U.S. and NATO troops start the ninth year of war, there is little progress to be shown. This year has proven to be the

Erik Leaver, "Decision Point: Afghanistan," Foreign Policy In Focus, October 1, 2009. Reproduced by permission.

most deadly for U.S. and coalition troops since the war began. Over 1,500 Afghan civilians have died this year and more than 450 Afghan security forces have died.

Sadly, the sacrifices these solders made have not resulted in better conditions for Afghans on the ground. Agricultural production is at its lowest since the war began, only 23% of the population has access to clean drinking water, and 40% lives below the poverty line. Life expectancy in Afghanistan is 44 years. Three million Afghans have fled their country. According to a UN [United Nations] threat assessment, 40% of Afghanistan is today either Taliban-controlled or a high-risk area for insurgent [rebel] attacks.

Beyond the human toll, the war is taking a severe financial hit on the United States. To date, the U.S. has spent more than $220 billion in Afghanistan. Over 90% of that spending has been for the military. Today, the U.S. is spending $4 billion a month in Afghanistan and has eclipsed the costs of Iraq for the first time.

But policy makers in Washington don't see Afghanistan being in crisis for these reasons. Instead, the focus is on the tension between the White House and the Department of Defense on two key questions: What is the proper mission for troops and should the United States send additional soldiers?

Few players in Washington are asking the most important questions, is there a role for troops at this point at all, what does an exit strategy look like and when can we get there?

The Request for More Troops

Running on a platform that stressed that Afghanistan was the "good war," President Obama not surprisingly authorized a troop increase for Afghanistan of 21,000 soldiers just two months into office. He made this decision on the heels of no less than eight strategy reviews conducted during the end of 2008 and beginning of 2009. Coupled with his troop increase, Obama issued his own five point plan in March focused on "a clear and focused goal: to disrupt, dismantle and defeat al-Qaeda in Pakistan and Afghanistan."

In May of 2009, Obama tapped General Stanley McChrystal to take over as commander of the forces in Afghanistan. Formerly head of Joint Special Operations Command, Mc-Chrystal came to the job with high marks for his role in directing the military's clandestine special operations in Iraq. When he came officially on board in June, McChrystal started yet another policy review.

Delivered to Obama on August 30, the review set off a firestorm at the White House and in the media. In part, the controversy revolved around the leaking of the classified report by *Washington Post* reporter Bob Woodward on September 20. But the real debate unfolded around McChrystal's statement that if he didn't get reinforcements his mission would "likely result in failure."

The report exposed an existing divide between the military and civilian policy makers, with the brass supporting McChrystal's assessment for more troops and the civilians wary of an escalation. But the leak deepened this divide, as controversy brewed about who leaked the report, and more importantly, why.

The divide over the next steps in Afghanistan extends outside of Washington as well with a new *USA Today* poll indicating that 50% of Americans oppose sending more troops to Afghanistan, a 15% drop in support from March, when Obama ordered more troops. And where perhaps it matters most, in Afghanistan, support is even lower. A February 2009 ABC/BBC/ARD poll found that only 18% of Afghans support increasing the number of U.S. troops in their country.

On September 26, a spokesperson confirmed that Mc-Chrystal submitted a formal request for more troops but refused to comment on the number of additional troops requested. However, estimates of McChrystal's request range from 10,000 to 45,000 troops. Paul Pillar, national intelligence

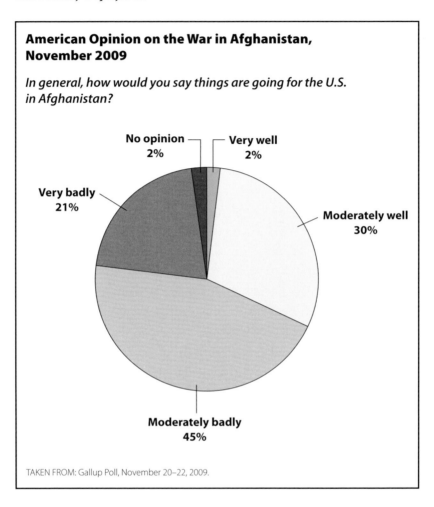

American Opinion on the War in Afghanistan, November 2009

In general, how would you say things are going for the U.S. in Afghanistan?

No opinion
2%

Very well
2%

Very badly
21%

Moderately well
30%

Moderately badly
45%

TAKEN FROM: Gallup Poll, November 20–22, 2009.

officer for the Near East and South Asia during the invasion of Afghanistan in 2001, dryly noted that if the administration requests the upper range then "the US will reach the level of the Russians at the peak of their deployment in the eighties: More than 100,000." [President Obama authorized 30,000 additional U.S. troops on December 1, 2009.] . . .

A No-Win Situation

But the question remains, even if McChrystal gets all of the troops he wants, is the mission possible? While it seems that a narrow mission that Obama proposed back in March to "disrupt, dismantle and defeat al-Qaeda in Pakistan and Afghanistan" could be within the grasp of the United States and NATO, McChrystal's counterinsurgency strategy seems unobtainable, even in his own review. He notes that the Afghan state is too weak to build the support needed for a robust counterinsurgency campaign and that NATO may not be well trained, equipped, or properly motivated for success.

Indeed, Afghanistan is causing many to question NATO's ability to last much beyond its 60th anniversary this year.

Furthermore, McChrystal's plan is highly dependent on the training of the Afghan National Army (ANA). Such training has been a dismal failure in the past eight years, even as the United States has spent $17.6 billion instructing the ANA. Saying that we now can do better is a dubious proposition at best. Rebuilding the Afghan military is no small task, no matter how many trainers McChrystal would like to send.[1]

The alternative suggested by many of the earlier strategic reviews and now championed by Vice President Joe Biden, is to narrow the mission to focus on al-Qaeda and the Taliban, essentially calling for action to stop Afghanistan from becoming a safe haven for terrorists. Indeed, this is the counterterrorism strategy that President [George W.] Bush pursued with little success. The problem with even this more limited objective is that the United States or NATO could not achieve it without staying in Afghanistan forever. As long as the United States and NATO forces are there in great numbers, it won't be claimed as a safe haven. But when forces leave, al-Qaeda would simply return.

The inertia of the last eight years is hard to overcome. In some sense, it's more difficult with Democrats both in the White House and running Congress. If Obama were to withdraw from Afghanistan and an attack occurred against the

---

1. McChrystal resigned from his commands in Afghanistan in June 2010 following unflattering remarks made about Obama administration officials that were attributed to McChrystal.

United States, the party fears that it would stand accused of being weak on defense for another 40 years. On the other side of the coin, doubling down on George Bush's war by sending more troops and resources has little chance of success. Even if it did succeed, such a strategy would likely further damage the U.S. economy, military, and our standing in the world in the process.

Another option is needed on the table—a clear and measurable timetable for withdrawal.

Avoiding the Graveyard of Empires

Afghanistan has been far too often called the "Graveyard of Empires." Although the reference applies to a much different time in the world, it may be applicable once again since the only two options under discussion would not likely bring a successful conclusion to the war. General McChrystal's plan offers no timetable or exit strategy, beyond warning that the next 12–18 months are critical—a timeframe that *New York Times* columnist Thomas Friedman bandied about so freely in Iraq that estimates like McChrystal's became known as "Friedman Units." And Secretary of Defense Robert Gates has rejected outright a timetable for withdrawal. But with NATO partners Britain, France, and Germany calling for a timeline, this option should be examined more closely.

The timetable that was set in Iraq indicates that such an approach can be useful in extricating the United States from a bad position. Most importantly, it begins to disarm the Taliban's argument that the "occupiers" will never leave. Calling for a timetable for withdrawal also recognizes that at some point Afghanistan, like Iraq and almost all other wars, will end with a negotiated peace treaty.

Figuring out what that treaty should say and constructing a timetable to meet those conditions should be the next step in Afghanistan. Given the lack of legitimacy for the [Afghan president Hamid] Karzai government and the relative political strength of the Taliban, negotiations must include a wide range of Afghans. Key principles for a treaty should include:

Deny al-Qaeda Safe Haven. Most analysts would argue that keeping Afghanistan (and other countries across the globe) free of al-Qaeda and terrorist networks should be a primary objective for global security. But the manner in which this can be achieved is under fierce debate. Occupation and options for open invasion whenever deemed necessary should be off the table. Instead, relying on the power in the United Nations Security Council and the provisions of Chapter VII provide nation states the opportunity to adequately protect themselves from imminent attack. Coupled with an international effort to track and capture members of terrorist networks, this should provide the United States and the international community with the strongest response possible. One primary example of this was the capture of [alleged Kuwaiti terrorist and al-Qaeda member] Khalid Sheikh Mohammed, who was not nabbed in a military raid but by combined police work.

Too much of the debate has focused on who rules Afghanistan and not on our goal of isolating al-Qaeda. The United States shouldn't try to determine who can be in the government, how it is chosen, or how it rules, so long as that government abides by an agreement not to harbor al-Qaeda, and to work with the international community to enforce that agreement. The Taliban itself is not a threat to the United States.

Commit to Development. Afghanistan is one of the most underdeveloped nations in the world. Funding for development so far has been far below needed levels. The country urgently needs basic infrastructure. Without roads, access to markets, better agricultural inputs, and available credit, local businesses can't start up or thrive. Such levels of commerce are needed to help combat the lucrative drug trade and raise the population out of poverty.

With few natural resources and a government highly dependent on international contributions, dedicated funding from the international community is needed. However, aid provided so far has not been successful. Too many projects are planned, designed, and implemented with far too little involvement from Afghans. Failure to learn from Greg Mortenson's book, *Three Cups of Tea*, where the success of Mortenson's development projects are dependent on working hand-in-hand with the local population, has doomed many of these projects. Aid should go directly to Afghan-led organizations, coupled with strong auditing by international agencies.

Withdraw All Combat Troops. Foreign troops on the ground (and drone attacks from the air) have been the biggest irritant to Afghan citizens and have been the most important tool for recruiting in terrorist networks. A commitment to withdrawing all combat troops will help deflate the recruitment for these groups. While growing the Afghan National Army is critical for the security of Afghanistan, the lack of human rights training, measures of accountability, and most important, a central government to report to, has severely undermined the legitimacy of these troops. Further training must be refocused and fall under a common set of guidelines, including oversight under the Leahy Law that suspends training funding for any groups involved in human rights abuses.

Separate Pakistan from Afghanistan. No essay on Afghanistan these days seems to omit the problems arising in Pakistan. It is wrong to see the distinct challenges facing these two countries as one struggle and the U.S. history in Pakistan requires a far different approach. The United States must address directly with Pakistan the flow of al-Qaeda and the Taliban into that country.

Clearly there are other steps to be taken, but these are the most important and should be the starting point for negotiations. As much as the citizens of United States and the world want President Obama to succeed in fixing Afghanistan, the policies that are under discussion are most likely to put us one more "Friedman Unit" away from a resolution. With more civilians and soldiers bound to perish during that time, it's time for a fundamentally different approach—one that can greatly diminish the greatest threats to the United States and at the same time, start Afghanistan on the road to recovery.

11

The U.S. Military Presence in Asia Has Been Key to Stability in the Region

William Breer

In the following viewpoint William Breer contends that the 60-year U.S.-Japan alliance has been critical to stability in Asia. He argues that the U.S. military presence in Japan and South Korea, along with alliances with other East Asian countries, has maintained peace in the region and helped economic growth. Despite periodic opposition to the U.S. military in Japan, South Korea, and elsewhere, Breer claims that the United States has been able to keep the alliances strong. He argues that it will be important for the United States to continue to maintain a strong alliance with Japan. Breer is senior advisor for the Center for Strategic & International Studies, an organization that provides strategic insights and policy solutions to decisionmakers in government, international institutions, the private sector, and civil society.

May 20 [2010] marks the 60th anniversary of the ratification of the U.S.-Japan alliance by Japan's House of Representatives. While the alliance is a bilateral arrangement, it has had a significant impact on Asia as a whole and is regarded by other nations as a key part of the regional security structure. The following is a brief survey of the treaty's role in the maintenance of peace and stability in the Asia-Pacific. It also demonstrates that the tensions currently confronting the U.S.-Japan alliance are not unique, but in fact have been faced

William Breer, "U.S. Alliances in East Asia: Internal Challenges and External Threats," Brookings Institution, May 2010. Reproduced by permission.

by various bilateral alliances in the region; some have been resolved successfully and some have not.

The U.S.-Japan Alliance

Most experts believe that the series of alliances the United States created after World War II was one of the most astute and far-sighted acts of diplomacy in history. The alliance with Japan laid the foundation for reconciliation between two enemy nations and the groundwork for the reconstruction of a nation whose industrial power, infrastructure, and morale lay in shambles, but which rose to become the world's second largest economy. The alliance, played a key role in the Cold War by allowing the United States to cover the USSR's [Union of Soviet Socialist Republics, or Soviet Union] eastern flank and demonstrating to China and North Korea that we would defend our interests and those of our allies in East Asia.

The arrangements with Japan provided a base from which the U.S. was able to defend its Republic of Korea [ROK, or South Korea] ally from aggression by the North. Although the Korean War ended in an armistice—not a victory for the ROK, U.S., and their allies—without the use of facilities in Japan the peninsula could have been lost. Another plus was that American protection relieved Japan of having to acquire an offensive military capability, possibly including nuclear weapons. This reassured Japan's neighbors that it would not again become a threat to their independence.

The result has been five decades of peace in Northeast Asia without a serious arms competition and remarkably few serious threats to the peace. This, along with the stimulus of Korean War procurement, enabled Japan to devote its resources to economic development, which resulted in a previously unimaginable economic expansion and improvement in living standards. The ROK, Taiwan, and later China, piggybacking on Japan's success and partaking of Japan's foreign aid and investment policies, replicated Japan's experience and delivered even faster rates of economic growth and prosperity to their people. None of this would have been possible without the American alliance system and the stability it provided throughout the region. The American presence in East Asia has been reassuring to allies, and our naval and air deployments beyond the region have played a major role in protecting the key energy trade routes through the Malacca Strait and Indian Ocean.

U.S. Foreign Military Bases

While the results have been good and generations of alliance managers on both sides can take considerable satisfaction in their accomplishments, the presence of foreign military bases in sovereign countries is not necessarily a natural phenomenon. Many Americans feel that we are motivated by altruism in undertaking to defend other peoples and that our actions are benign. But this view is not necessarily shared by citizens of host countries, many of whom view the American presence as an extension of the occupation in the case of Japan, an intrusion on sovereignty, or as a nuisance. These feelings are reinforced by a complex legal regime governing our bases and serious incidents (rape, hit-and-run accidents, etc.) involving American personnel. At the same time, as the base arrangements provide significant economic benefits for local populations there are some who welcome their presence. The policies of the new [Japanese prime minister Yukio] Hatoyama government reflect these contradictory views.

Governments have responded to these issues in different ways. In Japan we have developed mechanisms for dealing with problems and have accumulated a great deal of experience in working together. As a result Japanese citizens have tolerated a foreign military presence remarkably well. This may be a historic first. The leaderships of both nations realize the important role that the alliance plays in maintaining stability in East Asia and have striven to protect it.

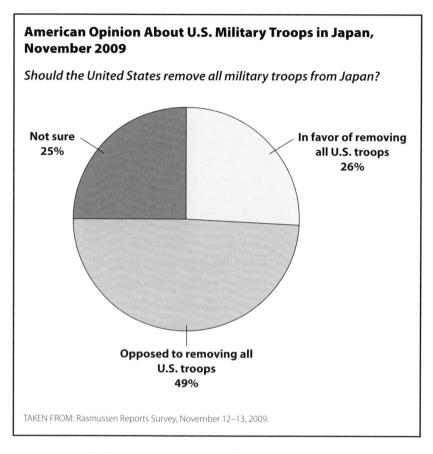

American Opinion About U.S. Military Troops in Japan, November 2009

Should the United States remove all military troops from Japan?

Not sure
25%

In favor of removing
all U.S. troops
26%

Opposed to removing all
U.S. troops
49%

TAKEN FROM: Rasmussen Reports Survey, November 12–13, 2009.

In the Philippines, where we had maintained major naval and air facilities for many decades, a combination of domestic political pressure, the destruction of one base by a volcanic eruption rendering it unusable, and a strategic reassessment in Washington resulted in the withdrawal of U.S. forces, but the continuation of the defense treaty. In recent years, small numbers of U.S. military advisors have assisted the Philippine armed forces in countering Muslim insurgents in the southern islands of Mindanao and the Sulu Archipelago.

Other U.S. Allies in East Asia

This was followed a few years later by the New Zealand government's refusal to allow port calls by U.S. Navy vessels, as clearly envisioned in the ANZUS [Australia, New Zealand, United States] treaty, without a prior finding by the prime minister of New Zealand that the ships in question were not carrying nuclear weapons. This was contrary to our long-standing policy of neither confirming nor denying the presence of nuclear weapons aboard our ships and put at risk our arrangements with Japan. The result was a suspension of our defense relationship with New Zealand and strained relations with this ally for a number of years. When the U.S. Navy revised its "neither confirm nor deny" policy, our defense relationship gradually improved. However, as Secretary of State George Shultz stated at the time of the break in 1986, "We remain friends, but we are no longer allies."

We do not have a security treaty with Taiwan and do not maintain forces on the island. We sell arms consistent with the terms of the Taiwan Relations Act and U.S. policy toward Taiwan has assured the people of Taiwan and other countries in the region that the United States takes the security of Taiwan seriously and that only a peaceful, non-coercive resolution of the political issues across the Taiwan Strait would be satisfactory.

Under our mutual defense treaty with the Republic of Korea we deploy sizable ground and air forces to the peninsula to backup ROK defenses in the event of aggression by North Korea. We have made clear to the North that the American commitment to the defense of South Korea is rock solid, and the peace has been maintained. While the U.S. posture has effectively deterred North Korea from a frontal attack, it has not prevented North Korea from mounting provocations, ranging from the capture of the *USS Pueblo* in 1968, through the tree-cutting incident in 1976, to the recent apparent sinking of an ROK warship. The biggest challenge posed by North Korea is its determination to acquire deployable nuclear weapons, which would threaten U.S. interests throughout East Asia, potentially pose an existential threat to Japan, and create a proliferation problem of vast proportions. Our treaty relationships with Japan and Korea, and our many decades of experience working together, have greatly facilitated our cooperation on this issue.

Dealing with Opposition

From time to time, base issues (one of our major bases is in the center of Seoul) and occasional incidents caused by American personnel have aroused latent nationalism among the people, which has in the past resulted in large scale demonstrations, strains in our relations with the host government, and pressure to relocate our facilities. That we are making necessary adjustments to our deployments without significantly reducing our support for the ROK or the effectiveness of our deterrent is a credit to the common sense and foresight of Korean and American officials, many of whom have devoted entire careers to the management of the defense of the ROK.

Australia has been a valued ally in a large number of military operations in which the U.S. has engaged over the last fifty years, despite periodic internal opposition to American policy.

Australia and Southeast Asia have been direct beneficiaries of America's alliance structure. While Australia is a member of ANZUS it has never become a platform for large scale American deployments. It has a keen interest in the stability and economic well-being of Northeast Asia because of its enormous and profitable economic ties with the region. It is also a beneficiary of American attention to the sea lanes to its West and North on which it depends for the bulk of its international commerce.

Despite periodic outbursts of opposition to nuclear ship home-porting or other aspects of the U.S. deployment in Japan, support among the Japanese people for the security relationship has remained at a remarkably high level. As a result the U.S. has had a relatively free hand in the use of our facilities and in the deployment of forces there. Generations of Japanese leaders have cooperated with U.S. security needs. These include a contribution of $13 billion in support of the first Gulf War, the dispatch of ground forces in support of our operations against Saddam Hussein, and generous foreign assistance to many places in which we have a strategic interest, including Afghanistan. Japan has also for the past 25 years made major contributions—$4–5 billion per year—to the support of U.S. forces in Japan. Who would have imagined 60 years ago that there would be significant U.S. military facilities in Japan in 2010?

The Future of the U.S.-Japan Alliance

The planned relocation of Marine Corps Air Station Futenma has posed major political issues for both Japan and the United States. Okinawa is host for the majority of U.S. forces in Japan and has endured the lion's share of the impact of foreign bases. Under considerable local pressure, Tokyo and Washington in 2006 reached an agreement to move the noisy Futenma facility from a densely populated area in central Okinawa to a sparsely populated region in the north. But the new Japanese administration, which took office in September 2009, ran on a platform calling for the removal of the facility from Okinawa. The U.S. side has been persistent in insisting that the agreement be implemented as it stands and relations have been seriously strained for more than half a year. But after much internal debate the prime minister has agreed that the original plan must go ahead.[1]

The decision to attack Iraq in 2003 and the sloppy execution of the war called into question American judgment and leadership. Uncertain progress in Afghanistan has compounded this. Neither of these has significantly weakened

---

1. Prime Minister Hayotama resigned on June 3, 2010, partly due to public outcry over retention of the U.S. military base at Okinawa. His successor, however, pledged that the Alliance with the U.S. would continue and the base would remain.

Japanese support for the alliance, but these creeping doubts, coupled with an increasingly inward-looking Japanese public, have helped create an era in which American strategic assessments and solutions will be viewed with greater skepticism. Another serious incident involving U.S. military personnel would put further strain on the relationship. This is not to say that we cannot cooperate on a wide range of issues, but such cooperation will require higher level USG [U.S. government] attention and a willingness on both sides to listen more attentively to the other's point of view. On the Japanese side, it will require the development of greater expertise among its political leaders and greater awareness among the general public of the changing environment. The increasing economic, military, and political importance of China demands that our two nations work together to assure a successful outcome in Asia.

12

Japan and South Korea Need a U.S. Military Presence

Matt Gurney

In the following viewpoint Matt Gurney argues that both Japan and South Korea need the military defense of the United States. He explains that in 2010 Japan backtracked in its opposition to the U.S. military presence there because of security concerns about North Korea. Similarly, Gurney says, South Korea is considering a delay for the removal of American forces in its country. He contends that the U.S. military presence in both countries is a necessity given the threat posed to Japan and South Korea by North Korea. Gurney is a member of the editorial board for the National Post, *a Canadian newspaper.*

Last week [June 3, 2010], Japanese prime minister Yukio Hatoyama resigned after barely eight months in office. Despite his desire to reduce Washington's influence over Japanese politics, Hatoyama was forced to back off a major campaign pledge—beginning the process of removing all American military forces from Japan's Okinawa Island. Already weakened by domestic political scandal, Hatoyama resigned rather than lead his Democratic Party into parliamentary elections next month. He felt that he had lost the confidence of his people after announcing that American forces would indeed be staying on Okinawa (though moving to a more remote location).

So ends the tenure of a man who came to power riding a wave of popularity, promising to lead Japan to a new era of

Matt Gurney, "Running Back to the U.S.A.," FrontPageMag.com, June 9, 2010. Reproduced by permission.

reduced spending and a foreign policy distinct from the United States. He ended Japan's supportive, non-combat role in the war in Afghanistan. His stated goal was to rebalance Japan's alliance with the United States, maintaining close ties, perhaps, but under terms less favorable to America.

The U.S. Military Presence in Japan

But now, he has quit, and his replacement has already sought to reassure America that the alliance will remain as-is. The reason for this sudden shift, yanking Japan firmly back into America's orbit, was explained by a joint statement issued by Tokyo and Washington: "Recent developments in the security environment of Northeast Asia reaffirmed the significance of the Alliance." Addressing reporters later, Hatoyama went further, saying, "I am painfully aware of the feeling of the people of Okinawa that the present problem of the bases represents unfair discrimination against them. At the same time, the presence of US bases is essential for Japan's security."

In other words, the North Koreans have rattled the Japanese. A year ago, Japan might have had reason to feel comfortable inching away from America, with the US military stretched and a new, dovish president seeking to avoid confrontations. But now with the North Koreans committing acts of war over and above their usual provocations, the Japanese have decided they'd rather keep their powerful friend around, after all. America's military faces an uncertain future during these times of fiscal duress and while the Democrats control both the White House and Congress, but the fact remains that it is still the world's best fighting force. Hatoyama, despite his earlier hopes of building a new Japan free of American protection and influence, has been forcefully reminded of just how dangerous a place the world can be.

The American presence on Okinawa Island, while essential for Japanese security in these turbulent times, is understandably an inconvenience for the local population. Okinawa is

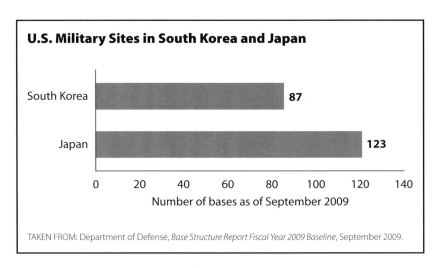

U.S. Military Sites in South Korea and Japan

South Korea — 87

Japan — 123

Number of bases as of September 2009

TAKEN FROM: Department of Defense, *Base Structure Report Fiscal Year 2009 Baseline*, September 2009.

small but densely populated: 1.3 million Japanese live on it, along with 25,000 Marines, plus their support staff and families. The forces housed on Okinawa represent fully half of the US forces stationed in Japan. In 1995, three Marines kidnapped and raped a 12-year-old girl. They were tried and sentenced to long prison terms, but the relationship between the US forces and the local Japanese population never recovered. When you factor in the petty crime, noise, pollution and crowding inherent to any large military force, it is easy to understand that the local civilians might resent the base. But the Marines' presence on Okinawa, setting aside such extremely rare incidents as the above-mentioned rape, is merely that—an inconvenience. America's support for Japan, in light of an aggressive North Korean regime capable of easily striking Japan, is a political and pragmatic necessity.

The U.S. Alliance with South Korea

The Japanese are not the only allies of the United States in the region to suddenly rediscover how beneficial a strong relationship with America can be. South Korea, the victim of North Korea's unprovoked attack, has enjoyed a long history of close defense relations with the United States, dating back to the Korean War itself, which saw American-led allied forces protect South Korea from North Korea communist forces, backed by Beijing and Moscow. For several years, however, the United States and South Korea have been working towards a transfer of control of all forces—including American—to South Korea. America has almost 30,000 troops in the South, but the South has a 600,000-man army. Under the new arrangement, the American troops would have taken a supporting role.

Since North Korea's attack, however, South Korea's defense community has become determined to delay the transfer of command. They do not want America to move into a supporting role—if war comes, they want to make very certain that US forces lead the charge against the numerically strong but technologically backwards North Korean military. The South Korean president is being pressured to invoke a clause in his country's alliance with the United States that would delay the planned 2012 handover of command to South Korea. Meanwhile, the utility of the alliance is being clearly demonstrated: despite the predictable outrage from the North, the United States plans to join South Korea in naval exercises in the weeks and months ahead, demonstrating the close relationship and military prowess of the allies to the troubled North. There has also been discussion of sending an American carrier battle group, and its awesome firepower, to the region to impress upon the North Koreans the wisdom of choosing a more peaceful course of action.

No decision to deploy the carrier has yet been made public, but the message is clear. For Japan and South Korea, the world can be a dangerous place. And in such a world, you can ask for no better friend than the United States of America.

13

The U.S. Military Forces Should Leave Japan

Doug Bandow

In the following viewpoint Doug Bandow argues that it is time for the United States to withdraw its military forces from Japan. He claims that the dependency of Japan on the United States created by the post–World War II treaty is now outdated. Responsibility for defending Japan lies with Japan, not the United States, Bandow asserts, despite the possible threats to Japan from its neighbors. He argues that the era of U.S. military dominance is coming to an end, and the United States should end its quasi-imperial role in the world beginning with a withdrawal of all military troops from Japan. Bandow is a senior fellow at the Cato Institute, specializing in foreign policy and civil liberties. He is co-author of The Korea Conundrum: America's Troubled Relations with North and South Korea.

World War II ended 65 years ago. The Cold War disappeared 21 years ago. Yet America's military deployments have little changed. Nowhere is that more evident than on the Japanese island of Okinawa.

The U.S.-Japan Defense Treaty

Okinawans are tired of the heavy U.S. military presence. Some 90,000—nearly 10 percent of the island's population—gathered in protest at the end of April [2010]. It is time for Washington to lighten Okinawa's burden.

Doug Bandow, "Japan Can Defend Itself," National Interest Online, May 12, 2010. Reproduced by permission.

An independent kingdom swallowed by imperial Japan, Okinawa was the site of a brutal battle as the United States closed in on Japan in early 1945. After Tokyo's surrender, Washington filled the main prefecture island with bases and didn't return it to Japan until 1972. America's military presence has only been modestly reduced since.

The facilities grew out of the mutual defense treaty between America and Japan, by which the former promised to defend the latter, which was disarmed after its defeat. The island provided a convenient home for American units. Most Japanese people also preferred to keep the U.S. military presence on Japan's most distant and poorest province, forcing Okinawans to carry a disproportionate burden of the alliance.

Whatever the justifications of this arrangement during the Cold War, the necessity of both U.S. ground forces in Japan and the larger mutual defense treaty between the two nations has disappeared. It's time to reconsider both Tokyo's and Washington's regional roles. The United States imposed the so-called "peace constitution" on Japan, Article 9 of which prohibits the use of force and even creation of a military.

However, American officials soon realized that Washington could use military assistance. Today's "Self-Defense Force" is a widely accepted verbal evasion of a clear constitutional provision.

Japan's Dependency on the United States

Nevertheless, both domestic pacifism and regional opposition have discouraged reconsideration of Japan's military role. Washington's willingness to continue defending an increasingly wealthy Japan made a rethink unnecessary.

Fears of a more dangerous North Korea and a more assertive People's Republic of China have recently increased support in Japan for a more robust security stance. The threat of piracy has even caused Tokyo to open its first overseas mili-

tary facility in the African state of Djibouti. Nevertheless, Japan's activities remain minimal compared to its stake in East Asia's stability.

Thus, Tokyo remains heavily dependent on Washington for its security. The then-opposition Democratic Party of Japan promised to "do away with the dependent relationship in which Japan ultimately has no alternative but to act in accordance with U.S. wishes." The party later moderated its program, calling for a "close and equal Japan-U.S. alliance."

However, the government promised to reconsider a previous agreement to relocate the Marines Corps Air Station at Futenma elsewhere on Okinawa. The majority of residents want to send the base elsewhere.

The [Barack] Obama administration responded badly, insisting that Tokyo fulfill its past promises. Only reluctantly did Washington indicate a willingness to consider alternatives—after imposing seemingly impossible conditions.

Still, the primary problem is Japan. So long as Tokyo requests American military protection, it cannot easily reject Washington's request for bases. Thus, Okinawan residents must do more than demand fairness. They must advocate defense independence.

The Japanese Duty of Defense

Who should protect Japan? Japan. Tokyo's neighbors remain uneasy in varying degrees about the prospect of a more active Japan, but World War II is over. A revived Japanese empire is about as likely as a revived Mongol empire. Both Japan and India could play a much larger role in preserving regional security.

Many Japanese citizens are equally opposed to a larger Japanese military and more expansive foreign policy. Their feelings are understandable, given the horrors of World War II. However, the most fundamental duty of any national government is defense. If the Japanese people want a minimal (or no) military, that is their right. But they should not expect other nations to fill the defense gap.

Moreover, with an expected $1.6 trillion deficit this year alone, the United States can no longer afford to protect countries which are able to protect themselves. Washington has more than enough on its military plate elsewhere in the world.

Raymond Greene, America's consul general in Okinawa, says: "Asia is going though a period of historic strategic change in the balance of power." True enough, which is why East Asian security and stability require greater national efforts from Japan and its neighbors. Regional defense also warrants improved multilateral cooperation—something which should minimize concerns over an increased Japanese role.

The Threats to Japan

The other important question is, defend Japan from what? Today Tokyo faces few obvious security threats. For this reason, many Japanese see little cause for an enlarged Japanese military.

However, North Korea's uncertain future and China's ongoing growth should give the Japanese people pause for concern. East Asia might not look so friendly in coming decades. Richard Lawless, assistant secretary of defense for Asian and Pacific security affairs in the [George W.] Bush administration, claimed: "Observers perceive a Japan that is seemingly content to marginalize itself, a Japan that appears to almost intentionally ignore the increasingly complex and dangerous neighborhood in which it is located." Nevertheless, only the Japanese can assess the threats which concern them rather than Washington. And only the Japanese can decide how best to respond to any perceived threats.

Moreover, so long as Japan goes hat-in-hand to the United States for protection, Washington is entitled to request—or, more accurately, insist on—bases that serve its interests. And Tokyo cannot easily say no.

Before the demonstration Prime Minister Yukio Hatoyama said that "It must never happen that we accept the existing plan." Afterwards he visited Okinawa and indicated that he planned to renege on his government's earlier promises: "We must maintain the Japan-U.S. alliance as a deterrent force, and . . . we must ask Okinawa to bear some of that burden." He added that, "It has become clear from our negotiations with the Americans that we cannot ask them to relocate the base to too far-flung a location." Apparently his government intends to move some facilities elsewhere on Okinawa as well as to the small island of Tokunoshima.

America's Quasi-Imperial Role

With Tokyo retreating from its commitment to chart a more independent course, it is up to the United States to reorder the relationship. Washington policy makers long have enjoyed America's quasi-imperial role. But U.S. citizens are paying for and dying in Washington's quasi-imperial wars. An expansive American role made sense during the Cold War in the aftermath of World War II. That world disappeared two decades ago.

Promiscuous intervention in today's world inflates the power of Washington policy makers but harms the interests of U.S. citizens. American forces and personnel are expected to be at perpetual risk guaranteeing the interests of other states, including Japan.

Thus the U.S. reliance on Okinawa. Lieutenant General Keith Stalder, the Marine Corps Pacific commander, said the island deployment is "the perfect model" for the alliance's objectives of "deterring, defending and defeating potential adversaries."

For years the most obvious target of the American forces was North Korea, with the 3rd Marine Expeditionary Force (MEF) expected to reinforce the Republic of Korea [ROK, or South Korea] in the event of war. Yet the ROK is both financially and manpower rich. More recently some Americans have talked about deploying the MEF to seize Pyongyang's nuclear weapons in the event of a North Korean collapse. Alas, so far the North has proved to be surprisingly resilient, so the Marines might wait a long time to undertake this mission.

Checking China is next on the potential Okinawa mission list. However, no one expects the United States to launch a ground invasion of the People's Republic of China irrespective of the future course of events. Thus, the MEF wouldn't be very useful in any conflict. In any case, a stronger Japanese military—which already possesses potent capabilities—would be a far better mechanism for encouraging responsible Chinese development.

There's also the kitchen sink argument: The Marines are to maintain regional "stability." Pentagon officials draw expanding circles around Okinawa to illustrate potential areas of operation.

The mind boggles, however. Should U.S. troops be sent to resolve, say, the long-running Burmese guerrilla war in that nation's east, a flare-up of secessionist sentiment in Indonesia, violent opposition to Fiji's military dictator, or border skirmishes between Cambodia and Thailand? It is hard to imagine any reason for Washington to jump into any local conflict. America's presumption should be noninvolvement rather than intervention in other nations' wars.

Making fewer promises to intervene would allow the United States to reduce the number of military personnel and overseas bases. A good place to start in cutting international installations would be Okinawa.

The End of American Dominance

America's post–Cold War dominance is coming to an end. Michael Schuman argued in *Time*: "Anyone who thinks the balance of power in Asia is not changing—and with it, the strength of the U.S., even among its old allies—hasn't been there lately."

Many analysts nevertheless want the United States to attempt to maintain its unnatural dominance. Rather than accommodate a more powerful China, they want America to contain a wealthier and more influential Beijing. Rather than expect its allies to defend themselves and promote regional stability, they want Washington to keep its friends dependent.

To coin a phrase, it's time for a change. U.S. intransigence [uncompromising position] over Okinawa has badly roiled the bilateral relationship. But even a more flexible basing policy would not be enough. Washington is risking the lives and wasting the money of the American people to defend other populous and prosperous states.

Washington should close Futenma—as a start to refashioning the alliance with Japan. Rather than a unilateral promise by the United States to defend Japan, the relationship should become one of equals working together on issues of mutual interest. Responsibility for protecting Japan should become that of Japan.

Both Okinawans and Americans deserve justice. It's time for Washington to deliver.

14

The U.S. Army Should Leave South Korea

Joshua Stanton

In the following viewpoint Joshua Stanton argues that the U.S. military ground presence in South Korea should end. Stanton claims that in South Korea there is rampant anti-Americanism and resentment of the U.S. Army forces, and that South Korea is not operating as an effective ally for the United States elsewhere. He also asserts that the U.S. subsidization of South Korean defense has prevented them from developing their own adequate defense, while also being counterproductive in North Korean disarmament. While not going as far as calling for the withdrawal of all U.S. military troops, Stanton concludes that it is time for the U.S. Army forces to leave South Korea. Stanton is an attorney practicing in Washington, D.C. He started the blog One Free Korea, that advocates for the human rights of the North Korean people.

The ground component of U.S. Forces Korea, which costs U.S. taxpayers billions of dollars a year to maintain, is an equally unaffordable political liability on the South Korean street. We should withdraw it. Every Saturday night off-post brawl is a headline in the muck-raking Korean press, for which the American soldier is inevitably blamed, and for which angry mobs perpetually demand renegotiations of the Status of Forces Agreement [SOFA] to give Korea's not-even-remotely-fair judicial system more jurisdiction over American soldiers.

Joshua Stanton, "It's Time for the U.S. Army to Leave Korea," *The New Ledger*, April 11, 2010. Reproduced by permission.

Anti-Americanism in South Korea

The South Korean people do not appreciate the security our soldiers provide. The way some of them treat our soldiers ought to be a national scandal. Many off-post businesses don't even let Americans through their front doors. The degree of anti-Americanism in South Korea is sufficient to be a significant force protection issue in the event of hostilities.

South Korea does not have our back. South Korea made much of the fact that it sent 3,000 soldiers to Iraq, where they sat behind concrete barriers in a secure Kurdish area of Iraq, protected by peshmerga [Kurdish fighters], making no military contribution and taking no combat casualties. Their contribution to the effort in Afghanistan has been negligible, which is more than can be said of their contribution to the Taliban (previous President Roh Moo Hyun reportedly paid them a ransom of up to $20 million in 2007 to free South Korean hostages who took it upon themselves to charter a shiny new bus to bring Christianity to Kandahar). South Korea has been an equally unsteady ally against China.

The American security blanket has fostered a state of national adolescence by the South Korean public. Too many of them (some polls suggest most) see America as a barrier to reunification with their ethnic kindred in the North. Maybe nothing short of a North Korean attack on the South can encourage more sober thinking by South Koreans about their own security, but I suspect a greater sense of self-reliance and even vulnerability might.

The Lack of South Korean Defense

During my service in Korea, as U.S. taxpayers subsidized South Korea's defense, South Korea subsidized [North Korea's supreme leader] Kim Jong Il's potential offense with billions of dollars in hard currency that sustained the very threat against which we were ostensibly helping to defend. South Korea never made North Korea's disarmament a condition of this aid. Instead, that aid effectively undermined U.S. and U.N. [United Nations] sanctions meant to force North Korea to disarm. What does South Korea have to show for this colossal outlay now?

Because South Korea, now one of the world's wealthiest nations, expects up to 600,000 American soldiers to arrive to protect it from any security contingency, successive South Korean governments actually cut their nation's defense rather than modernizing it and building an effective independent defense. Consequently, South Korea still has a 1970-vintage force structure, designed around a 1970-vintage threat, equipped with 1970-vintage weapons.

This is partly the legacy of ten years of leftist administrations, but it's also the legacy of military welfare that allowed South Korea to defer upgrading its equipment, building a professional volunteer army, and organizing an effective reserve force to deal with security contingencies. Worst of all, South Korea diverted billions of dollars that should have been spent on modernizing its military into regime-sustaining aid to Kim Jong Il, to be used, as far as anyone knows, for nukes, missiles, artillery, and pretty much everything but infant formula. To this day, South Korea continues to resist accepting operational control over its own forces in the event of war.

An Anachronistic Presence

The U.S. Army presence in Korea is an anachronism, defending against the extinct threat of a conventional North Korean invasion. The far greater danger is that if Kim Jong Il assesses our current president [Barack Obama] as weak, he will choose more limited or less conventional means to strike at our soldiers and their families. Given the reported presence of Taliban operatives in Seoul, he might even plausibly deny responsibility for an attack.

Thus, while I don't go so far as to accept the *Princess Bride* Doctrine ("never get involved in a land war in Asia"), I do not believe it is wise for us to have our forces within easy artillery range of Kim Jong Il, such that he may freely choose the time, place, and manner of our involvement. . . .

This is not to suggest that we unilaterally abrogate [nullify] the alliance with South Korea. Our air and naval installations in Korea provide useful power-projection capability and are far more secure, ironically, than our many scattered and isolated Army posts.

111

I can imagine any number of contingencies for which we'd want to have the ability to move people and supplies into South Korea in a hurry.

Facts About U.S. Military Deployment

U.S. Military Bases Abroad

According to the U.S. Department of Defense (DoD), there are 716 DoD sites owned or managed overseas as of September 2009. (Sites in Iraq and Afghanistan are not included, since the military sites there are part of an active war of aggression and not semi-permanent sites set up by treaty or agreement with a government body.) By division of the U.S. Armed Forces:

- 293 U.S. Army sites
- 261 U.S. Air Force sites
- 136 U.S. Navy sites
- 26 Marine Corps sites

By size (according to Plant Replacement Value, or PRV):

- 13 large sites (PRV greater than or equal to $1.69 billion)
- 261 U.S. Air Force sites
- 19 medium sites (PRV less than $1.69 billion and greater than or equal to $901 million)
- 620 small sites (PRV less than $901 million)
- 261 U.S. Air Force sites
- 64 other sites (PRV equal to 0)

By country (those that have at least 10 sites):

- Germany—235 sites
- Japan—123 sites
- South Korea—87 sites
- Italy—83 sites
- United Kingdom—47 sites

- Portugal—21 sites
- Turkey—19 sites
- Belgium—18 sites

Overall statistics on sites overseas:
- 29,648 buildings owned and 4,968 leased
- 244,453 acres owned of 634,919 total acres used
- Plant Replacement Value (PRV) for all sites = $124.2 billion
- 1,814,543 military personnel and 490,454 authorized civilian personnel

U.S. Military Presence in Japan

The 1951 Security Treaty Between the United States and Japan following the end of World War II established the right of the United States to have military forces in Japan.
- Article 1 of the Security Treaty Between the United States and Japan states, "Japan grants, and the United States of America accepts, the right . . . to dispose United States land, air and sea forces in and about Japan."
- The 1960 U.S.–Japan Treaty of Mutual Cooperation and Security replaced the 1951 treaty, but continued the U.S. military presence under Article 6, which states, "the United States of America is granted the use by its land, air and naval forces of facilities and areas in Japan."
- At the end of 2009, 35,688 troops were stationed at the 123 U.S. military bases in Japan.

U.S. Military Presence in South Korea

The 1953 U.S.–R.O.K. Mutual Defense Treaty following the end of the Korean War established the ability of the United States to have military bases in the Republic of Korea (R.O.K., or South Korea) in order to help R.O.K. defend itself.

- Article 4 of the U.S.–R.O.K. Mutual Defense Treaty states, "The Republic of Korea grants, and the United States of America accepts, the right to dispose United States land, air and sea forces in and about the territory of the Republic of Korea as determined by mutual agreement."

- The United States and R.O.K. made an agreement in 2008 that caps the number of troops at the 87 U.S. military bases in R.O.K. at 28,500.

Iraq War

The current Iraq War, also known as the Second Gulf War or Operation Iraqi Freedom, began on March 30, 2003, led by forces of the United States and United Kingdom. In February 2009, the United States announced it would begin withdrawing forces, with all U.S. troops planned to be out of Iraq by the end of 2011.

- According to the Department of Defense, at the end of 2009, there were 151,000 troops deployed in and around Iraq (including Kuwait).

- As of July 27, 2010, CNN reported 4,733 U.S. and Coalition forces casualties and 31,888 wounded since the start of the war.

- According to the Brookings Institution, the estimated number of Iraqi civilian deaths from the start of the war through June 15, 2010, was approximately 100,000.

- According to the National Priorities Project, the cost of the war in Iraq through June 2010 is over $730 billion. The cost for fiscal year 2010 is over $64 billion.

Afghanistan War

The current war in Afghanistan, known as Operation Enduring Freedom, began on October 7, 2001, in response to the September 11th attacks on the United States; the war was launched by forces of the United States and United Kingdom. In December 2009, the United States announced it would escalate involvement by deploying an additional 30,000 troops, with plans to begin withdrawing troops eighteen months later.

- According to the Department of Defense, at the end of 2009, there were 71,000 troops deployed in and around Afghanistan.

- As of July 27, 2010, CNN reported 1,956 U.S. and Coalition forces casualties and 7,011 wounded.

- According to the United Nations Assistance Mission in Afghanistan (UNAMA), the estimated number of Afghani civilian deaths in 2009 was 2,412, a 14 percent increase over the 2,118 deaths recorded in 2008.

- According to the National Priorities Project, the cost of the war in Afghanistan through June 2010 is over $280 billion. The cost for fiscal year 2010 is over $72 billion.

Organizations to Contact

The editors have compiled the following list of organizations concerned with the issues debated in this book. The descriptions are derived from materials provided by the organizations. All have publications or information available for interested readers. The list was compiled on the date of publication of the present volume; the information provided here may change. Be aware that many organizations take several weeks or longer to respond to inquiries, so allow as much time as possible.

American Enterprise Institute (AEI)
1150 Seventeenth Street NW, Washington, DC   20036
(202) 862-5800 • Fax: (202) 862-7177
E-mail: info@aei.org
Web site: www.aei.org

AEI is a private, nonpartisan, nonprofit institution dedicated to research and education on issues of government, politics, economics, and social welfare. AEI sponsors research and publishes materials toward the end of defending the principles of American freedom and democratic capitalism, through projects such as its Center for Defense Studies. AEI publishes *The American*, a bimonthly magazine, and a series of papers in its Economic Outlook series.

American Foreign Policy Council (AFPC)
509 C St. NE, Washington, DC   20002
(202) 543-1006 • Fax: (202) 543-1007
E-mail: afpc@afpc.org
Web site: www.afpc.org

AFPC is a nonprofit organization dedicated to bringing information to those who make or influence the foreign policy of the United States. AFPC provides resources to members of Congress, the executive branch, and the policy-making community. AFPC publishes policy papers and numerous in-house bulletins, including *China Reform Monitor*, *Eurasia Security Watch*, and *Iran Democracy Monitor*.

Brookings Institution
1775 Massachusetts Ave. NW, Washington, DC   20036
(202) 797-6000
E-mail: communications@brookings.edu
Web site: www.brookings.edu

The Brookings Institution is a nonprofit public policy organization that conducts independent research. The Brookings Institution uses its research to provide recommendations that advance the goals of strengthening American democracy, fostering social welfare and security, and securing a cooperative international system. The Brookings Institution publishes a variety of books, reports, and several journals, including the book *Toughing It Out in Afghanistan.*

Cato Institute
1000 Massachusetts Ave. NW, Washington, DC   20001-5403
(202) 842-0200 • Fax: (202) 842-3490
Web site: www.cato.org

The Cato Institute is a public policy research foundation dedicated to limiting the role of government, protecting individual liberties, and promoting free markets. The Cato Institute works to originate, advocate, promote, and disseminate applicable policy proposals that create free, open, and civil societies in the United States and throughout the world. Among the Cato Institute's many publications is the white paper "Escaping the 'Graveyard of Empires': A Strategy to Exit Afghanistan."

Center for Defense Information (CDI)
1779 Massachusetts Ave. NW, Washington, DC   20036-2109
(202) 332-0600 • Fax: (202) 462-4559
E-mail: info@cdi.org
Web site: www.cdi.org

CDI is an organization that works to promote discussion and debate on security issues such as nuclear weapons, space security, missile defense, and military transformation. CDI provides expert analysis on various components of U.S. national security, international security, and defense policy. CDI publishes reports, newsletters, *The Defense Monitor*, and books such as *Military Almanac 2007*.

Center for Security Policy
1901 Pennsylvania Ave. NW, Suite 201
Washington, DC   20006
(202) 835-9077 • Fax: (202) 835-9066
E-mail: info@centerforsecuritypolicy.org
Web site: www.centerforsecuritypolicy.org

The Center for Security Policy is a nonprofit, nonpartisan organization that works to establish successful national security policies through the use of diplomatic, informational, military, and economic strength. Through its research, the Center for Security Policy aims to identify policies, actions, and resource needs that are vital to American security. The Center for Security Policy publishes the weekly *Policy Decision Briefs*, the weekly *The Americas Report*, and occasional papers, all of which are available at its Web site.

Center for Strategic and International Studies (CSIS)
1800 K St. NW, Washington, DC   20006
(202) 887-0200 • Fax: (202) 775-3199
Web site: www.csis.org

CSIS is a nonprofit organization that provides strategic insights and bipartisan policy solutions to decision makers. CSIS conducts research and analysis for decision makers in government, international institutions, the private sector, and civil society. Among its many publications are the reports "A Key to Success in Afghanistan: A Modern Silk Road Strategy" and "Iraq and the United States," both available at its Web site.

Foreign Policy Research Institute (FPRI)
1528 Walnut St., Suite 610, Philadelphia, PA   19102
(215) 732-3774 • Fax: (215) 732-4401
E-mail: fpri@fpri.org
Web site: www.fpri.org

FPRI is an independent, nonprofit organization devoted to bringing the insights of scholarship to bear on the development of policies that advance U.S. national interests. FPRI conducts research on pressing issues and provides public education on international affairs. The organization publishes the quarterly *Orbis*, several periodical bulletins, and numerous essays, all of which are available at its Web site.

Institute for Foreign Policy Analysis (IFPA)

1725 DeSales St. NW, Suite 402, Washington, DC   20036-4406
(202) 463-7942 • Fax: (202) 785-2785
E-mail: dcmail@ifpa.org
Web site: www.ifpa.org

IFPA is an independent, nonpartisan research organization specializing in national security, foreign policy, and defense planning issues. IFPA helps senior government policy makers, industry leaders, and officials in the public policy community make decisions about global security. IFPA publishes numerous reports, including "Realigning Priorities: The U.S.-Japan Alliance and the Future of Extended Deterrence" and "Finding the Right Mix: Disaster Diplomacy, National Security, and International Cooperation."

Institute for Policy Studies (IPS)

1112 16th St. NW, Suite 600, Washington, DC   20036
(202) 234-9382
E-mail: info@ips-dc.org
Web site: www.ips-dc.org

IPS is a think tank that acts as a policy and research resource for progressive movements such as the anti-war movement. A project of the IPS, Foreign Policy in Focus, connects research and action of scholars, advocates, and activists seeking to make the United States a more responsible global partner. IPS publishes numerous reports available at its Web site, such as "Military vs. Climate Security: Mapping the Shift from the Bush Years to the Obama Era" and "The Cost of the Global U.S. Military Presence."

International Network for the Abolition of Foreign Military Bases

De Wittenstraat 25, 1052 AK Amsterdam, The Netherlands
(+31) 20-6626608 • Fax: (+31) 20-6757176
E-mail: secretariat@no-bases.net
Web site: www.no-bases.org

The International Network for the Abolition of Foreign Military Bases (or No-Bases Network) is a Dutch nonprofit organization working to eliminate foreign military bases around the world. The No-Bases Network provides information on U.S. and European military facilities worldwide and supports local struggles to abolish foreign military bases. The Web site of the International Network for the Abolition of Foreign Military Bases contains videos, maps, and documents about foreign military bases.

U.S. Department of Defense

1400 Defense Pentagon, Washington, DC   20301-1400
(703) 571-3343
Web site: www.defense.gov

The U.S. Department of Defense is the federal department that supervises all agencies of the government related to national security and the U.S. armed forces. Among those agencies are the Departments of Army, Navy, and Air Force; and the National Security Agency. The Web site of the U.S. Department of Defense contains news releases, photo essays, and reports, including the report "Measuring Stability and Security in Iraq March 2010."

Bibliography

Books

Michael R. Auslin *Voting with Dollars: A New Paradigm for Campaign Finance.* Cambridge, MA: Harvard University Press, 2006.

Andrew J. Bacevich *The Limits of Power: The End of American Exceptionalism.* New York: Metropolitan Books, 2009.

Stephen D. Biddle *Military Power: Explaining Victory and Defeat in Modern Battle.* Princeton, NJ: Princeton University Press, 2006.

John Bolton *Surrender Is Not an Option: Defending America at the United Nations and Abroad.* New York: Threshold Editions, 2008.

Kent E. Calder *Embattled Garrisons: Comparative Base Politics and American Globalism.* Princeton, NJ: Princeton University Press, 2007.

Alexander Cooley *Base Politics: Democratic Change and the U.S. Military Overseas.* Ithaca, NY: Cornell University Press, 2008.

Thomas Donnelly and Frederick Kagan, eds. *Lessons for a Long War: How America Can Win on New Battlefields.* Washington, DC: AEI Press, 2010.

Tom Engelhardt *The American Way of War: How the Empire Brought Itself to Ruin.* Chicago, IL: Haymarket Books, 2010.

Mark L. Gillem — *American Town: Building the Outposts of Empire*. Minneapolis: University of Minnesota Press, 2007.

Chalmers Johnson — *Dismantling the Empire: America's Last Best Hope*. New York: Metropolitan Books, 2010.

Robert D. Kaplan — *Hog Pilots, Blue Water Grunts: The American Military in the Air, at Sea, and on the Ground*. New York: Random House, 2008.

Catherine Lutz, ed. — *The Bases of Empire: The Global Struggle Against U.S. Military Posts*. New York: New York University Press, 2009.

Michael Mandelbaum — *The Case for Goliath: How America Acts as the World's Government in the Twenty-First Century*. New York: Public Affairs, 2005.

Jack F. Matlock, Jr. — *Superpower Illusions: How Myths and False Ideologies Led America Astray—and How to Return to Reality*. New Haven, CT: Yale University Press, 2010.

Rajan Menon — *The End of Alliances*. New York: Oxford University Press, 2007.

Kenneth M. Pollack — *A Path Out of the Desert: A Grand Strategy for America in the Middle East*. New York: Random House, 2009.

Christopher A. Preble	*The Power Problem: How American Military Dominance Makes Us Less Safe, Less Prosperous, and Less Free.* Ithaca, NY: Cornell University Press, 2009.
David S. Sorenson	*Military Base Closure: A Reference Handbook.* Westport, CT: Praeger Security International, 2007.
Stephen M. Walt	*Taming American Power: The Global Response to U.S. Primacy.* New York: Norton, 2005.

Periodicals and Internet Sources

Michael Auslin	"The Real Futenma Fallout," *Wall Street Journal*, June 16, 2010.
David Axe, Malou Innocent, and Jason Reich	"Defining Victory to Win a War," *Foreign Policy*, October 6, 2009.
Andrew J. Bacevich and Matthew A. Shadle	"No Exit from Iraq?" *Commonweal*, October 12, 2007.
Doug Bandow	"Recognizing the Limits of American Power in Afghanistan," *Huffington Post*, October 31, 2009.
Peter Bergen	"Winning the Good War: Why Afghanistan Is Not Obama's Vietnam," *Washington Monthly*, July–August 2009.

Stephen Biddle, Michael O'Hanlon, and Kenneth M. Pollack	"U.S. Troops Not Quite Ready to Go Home from Iraq," *New York Times*, August 5, 2008.
Tony Blankley	"The Afghanistan War Is a Farce," *National Review Online*, June 16, 2010.
John Bolton	"Should the United States Act with Humility in International Affairs?" *In Character*, March 3, 2010.
Thomas Donnelly	"Two Cheers for the U.S. Empire!" *New Statesman*, July 30, 2009.
Ivan Eland	"The U.S. Military Presence in South Korea Is Not a Model for Iraq," *American Chronicle*, June 11, 2007.
Tom Engelhardt	"Afghanistan: Too Big to Fail?" *Nation*, November 16, 2009.
Dexter Filkins	"Stanley McChrystal's Long War," *New York Times Magazine*, October 14, 2009.
Benjamin H. Friedman, Harvey Sapolsky, and Christopher Preble	"Learning the Right Lessons from Iraq," Cato Institute, *Policy Analysis*, February 13, 2008.
Leon T. Hadar	"The Moral Hazard of U.S. Global Interventions," *Huffington Post*, December 18, 2009.

Joshua Hammer · · · · · "Digging In," *Mother Jones*, March–April 2005.

Selig S. Harrison · · · · "How to Exit Afghanistan," *Nation*, January 11, 2010.

Chalmers Johnson · · · "Another Battle of Okinawa," *Los Angeles Times*, May 6, 2010.

Chalmers Johnson · · · "America's Unwelcome Advances: The Pentagon's Foreign Overtures Are Running into a World of Public Opposition," *Mother Jones*, August 22, 2008.

Frederick W. Kagan · · · · · · · · · · · "Afghanistan Is Not Vietnam," *Newsweek*, February 11, 2009.

Frederick W. Kagan and William Kristol · · · · · · · · · · "No Substitute for Victory," *Weekly Standard*, November 30, 2009.

Robert D. Kaplan · · · · "Saving Afghanistan," *Atlantic*, March 2009.

Michael T. Klare · · · · "Imperial Reach," *Nation*, April 25, 2005.

Christopher Layne · · · · · · · · · · · "Balancing Act: The U.S. Could Be More Secure by Doing Less," *American Conservative*, September 10, 2007.

Mark R. Levin · · · · · · "Not So Fast," *National Review Online*, September 4, 2009.

Jane C. Loeffler · · · · · "Fortress America," *Foreign Policy*, September–October 2007.

Justin Logan   "Argue Like It's 1991," *American
                      Conservative*, December 17, 2007.

Andrew   "A Dangerous Delusion: We Go to
McCarthy   War to Defend Our Interests, Not to
                     Encourage Democracy," *National
                     Review Online*, September 4, 2009.

Robert W.   "Why We Must Withdraw from Iraq,"
McElroy   *America*, April 30, 2007.

Mike Mochizuki   "Refocusing the U.S.–Japan Alliance:
and Michael   It's Not Just About an Air Base,"
O'Hanlon   *Washington Times*, December 18,
                     2009.

Michael E.   "Divide, and Be Conquered," *Los
O'Hanlon   Angeles Times*, March 3, 2010.

Onur Ozlu   "Iraqi Economic Reconstruction and
                     Development," *Center for Strategic
                     and International Studies*, April 21,
                     2006.

Kenneth M.   "Could We Still Lose Iraq?" *Daily
Pollack   Beast*, December 21, 2009.

Christopher A.   "Time to Leave," *USA Today*,
Preble   December 2, 2009.

John Shattuck   "Healing Our Self-Inflicted Wounds,"
                     American Prospect, January–February
                     2008.

Erik Swabb   "The U.S. Needs to Stay in Iraq,"
                     Boston Globe, March 20, 2007.

Paul Wolfowitz   "Think Again: Realism," *Foreign
                     Policy*, September–October 2009.

Index

A

Afghanistan, *74*
    Afghan deaths, 80
    American and Afghan public
      opinion about troop surge,
      81, *82*
    Bush strategy, 83
    democracy, 28
    economy, 77, 80
    exit strategy needed, 79–88
    history of foreign intervention
      in, 38–39, 84
    long-term, expanded U.S.
      commitment needed, 73–78
    number of troops deployed, 7
    Obama strategy, 39, 80, 82–83
    R.O.K. forces, 110
    staging bases for, 11
    Taliban, 29, 39, 75, 80
Afghanistan (Dupree), 39
Aggression against U.S. interests,
    retrenchment emboldens, 24
Al-Qaeda
    Obama goal, 80–81, 83, 85
    Pakistan and, 31–32, 79
Albright, Madeleine, 69
Anderson, Gary, 57
ANZUS treaty, 92, 93
Arguments against military
    facilities/deployments, 17–19
    commitment becomes endless,
      62–65, 79–88
    economic, 18, 34–38, 43, 49,
      103
    human rights, 46
    is anachronistic, 110–112

    leads to hatred of U.S., 19–21,
      50–55
Arguments for military facilities/
    deployments, 17–18
    in Afghanistan, 73–78
    humanitarian, 30–32
    maintenance of U.S. primacy
      of power, 27–33, 75
    peacekeeping, 60, 89, 96–99
    prevention of nuclear prolif-
      eration, 89
    safeguard U.S. interests, 24
    spread democracy, 28–29, 61
Armed Forces
    basic statistics, 7
    deployment statistics, 11–12,
      35
    training, 16–17
Arms exports, 43–44
Asia, 89–90, 103–106
    See also specific countries
Australia, 93

B

Balad Airbase, 12
Bandow, Doug, 100–107
Barr, Jay, 37
Benedict, Helen, 42
*Beyond the Green Zone: Dispatches
    from an Unembedded Journalist
    in Occupied Iraq* (Jamail), 42
Biden, Joe, 83
Bilateral agreements, 13
Breer, William, 88–95
Britain
    in Afghanistan, 38–39